I0624198

FINDING
HOPE
and HEALING
AFTER LOSING A CHILD

FINDING HOPE

and HEALING

AFTER LOSING A CHILD

Christian Stories of Faith and Family

SUSAN M. MESSICK
RAYMOND O. MESSICK

Published by Elemental Truth Publishing Company

Copyright © 2023 by Raymond O. Messick

All rights reserved. No part of this book may be used or reproduced in any manner whatsoever without written permission from the publisher, except in the case of brief quotations embodied in critical articles and reviews. This book has been registered with the U.S. Copyright Office.

Scripture quotations are from The ESV® Bible (The Holy Bible, English Standard Version®), copyright © 2001 by Crossway, a publishing ministry of Good News Publishers. Used by permission. All rights reserved.

Paperback ISBN: 979-8-9889378-0-7
Ebook ISBN: 979-8-9889378-1-4

Elemental Truth Publishing Company
5047 W Main Street, Ste 150
Kalamazoo, MI 49009

Address all inquiries to:
Raymond O. Messick
5047 W Main Street, Ste 150
Kalamazoo, MI 49009

Contents

Raymond's Stories

Dedication

From His Mother

This book is dedicated to
my only child and precious son:

Evan Michael Messick
July 13, 1998—February 3, 2009

Looking back over the years that I had Evan in my life, I found that my time being with him was about loving a child unconditionally, and not just having a baby. It was about developing the talents he had, not focusing on his limitations; the things I learned from knowing him, not what I could teach him; the puddles we splashed in together, not the rain that fell on us; the music we listened to, not the words he couldn't sing; the adventure of living in his world, not him trying to live in mine; moving forward with courage, not dwelling over what could not be changed; being happy while living in the present, and not worrying about the unknown future.

Dedication

To My Family

This book is dedicated to my only son and his mother:

Evan Michael Messick

July 13, 1998—February 3, 2009

Susan Marie Messick

May 13, 1956—July 3, 2014

For my handsome little boy Evan, whom I loved so very much, and waited for so long to be born: I have written this to honor and remember our time together. My plan to stay home with you until your 4th birthday was changed with the discovery of your health problems just after your 2nd birthday. Throughout your life, my priority was your health, safety, and of course, entertainment! Our morning stroller rides became wagon rides which became hand in hand walks together through our neighborhood and the adjoining neighborhood. We played together all day long: with tiny toys and books when you sat in your high chair; with toys requiring physical effort like your floor gym, doorway jumper, rocking horse, Gymnic HOP!66 ball, and the largest 9-foot-long tunnel by Pacific Play Tents, which was big enough for me to chase you through the tunnel at full speed.

We played with three sets of big multi-colored alphabet letters, and you were learning to spell words at a surprisingly early age. I frequently went to the bookstore to buy more books: board books of all kinds and sizes and lift-the-flap books were your early favorites, and you always read them.

Television was not allowed until you were one and a half years old. We were both introduced to Barney about this time, and you were a big fan. Barney & Friends became very useful later when you became ill with leukemia, and we had to spend weeks or even months in the hospital before we went home.

Throughout your life, you were a cheerful and happy boy who cooperated with the doctors and nurses trying to help you fight leukemia. You enjoyed going to school, and wanted to stay for the entire day even when you were not feeling well. All your doctors, nurses, and teachers loved and admired you.

For my amazing and wonderful wife Susan, whom I truly loved: I teased you on the day that we were married and said that it was your duty to outlive me, and you promised that you would. As things turned out, it was the only promise that you didn't keep. Faith and family were the most important things in your life, and you were always faithful and loving to me and Evan.

I always admired the remarkable range of interests and talents that you possessed. You graduated with a degree in Graphic Art from the American Academy of Art in Chicago. You had a keen eye for color and composition, and enjoyed capturing the natural world by painting beautiful landscapes using acrylic or oil on canvas. We were both very interested in photography. You would view an outdoor scene with a different perspective, and usually came home from our trips with pictures that I didn't remember seeing, even though we had walked the same paths around the lakes and waterfalls.

I was the top student in my English Composition class in college, but you were the one who wrote beautiful poetry that I could never write: you were far more creative than I.

I loved music and subscribed to five different magazines about home theater equipment, and teased you with pictures of speakers as big as refrigerators; but you had the talent to play the piano beautifully, and I used to love listening to you play for hours on Sunday afternoons.

Your intelligence, creativity, and powers of observation were put to work in the volatile world of finance. You started in Retail Mortgage Banking, and later switched to Wholesale Mortgage Banking. You worked for some of the major players in the Atlanta-Southeast Region and became one of the top Operations Managers. Your creative problem-solving abilities were used to fix situations at both the branch and corporate levels, and you were promoted to Assistant Vice-President, and later to National Wholesale Operations Manager.

Your ingenious wit and razor-sharp sense of humor were ever-present elements in any conversation; also, the fact that you could just look at me and know that I was up to something was always a problem. No one else could ever do that to me.

One night I was reading an online article about the human eye and its sensitivity to different colors of light. The professor knew that his article was highly technical and boring, so he put a series of humorous statements on each page, with the advice to read a few of them, and then return to his lecture.

One of the humorous statements caught my attention, and it was taken from the Old Testament book of Proverbs. Susan was sitting on the sofa in the great room, so I went into the great room with the printed article to share it with her. She looked at me and instantly knew that I looked a little too pleased with myself, so she just sat and waited to hear what I had come up with this time. I told her about the article, and then I read the quote to her: "It is better to live on a corner of the roof than to share a house with a quarrelsome wife." Without any hesitation, Susan said, "It's really cold outside. Better take two blankets when you crawl up on the roof."

What was I supposed to say to that? I just shook my head, turned around, and walked back to my home office as her laughter echoed down the hallway.

I loved Evan and Susan with all my heart, and because of the grace given to me by faith in Jesus Christ, I will see them again in the future, as He has promised.

Introduction

From His Mother

This is the book that I never thought I would write for the parents who never thought they would read it.

When my son died, I tried to find a book that would help me get through this situation. I went on the internet and searched for books, but couldn't find what I really wanted.

I could have left such an incredibly sensitive topic for someone else to address, but I decided to write this book. Having lived through it myself, I wanted to share what I have learned with other parents who lost their child.

My experiences, and the experiences of my family and friends, illustrate that we are not alone in the world. We are loved and watched over by God, our Heavenly Father, as well as our loved ones who have gone before us. Love does not end, and life does indeed go on. I believe that this book will help you find hope and healing after losing your child.

CHAPTER 1

On His Way Home

Some experiences in life can really open your eyes, and this one opened mine. On March 20, 1997, my mother called me from my northern Michigan hometown to tell me that my grandfather had died in his sleep that morning. The funeral would take place four days later on the next Monday.

I was saddened, but not surprised by this news. Grandpa had dealt with heart problems for the past thirty years, but modern medicine had allowed him to live to age 93. He had been very frail during his last five years, and was unable to do the things that he had enjoyed for most of his life. He was the youngest of thirteen children, and the last one to pass away.

Grandpa married my grandmother in 1929. They were married for 67 years, and raised seven children who gave them twenty-two grandchildren. Everyone loved him.

My family lived only three miles down the road from my grandparents. My brothers, sisters, and I were their first grandchildren, and we were very close to our grandparents. They gave us our roots, and the confidence to do our best.

When I was in my late twenties and still single, I decided to move to Atlanta for a new job opportunity. My family was now almost a thousand miles away. I missed them very much, and went back to visit whenever I could. Two years later, I married Ray, and we started our life together. Somehow, ten years just flew by.

Now I needed to go back to Michigan and pay my last respects to my grandfather. I was managing an extremely busy office in Atlanta that was understaffed, our personal finances were very tight, and airline fares had skyrocketed.

A year had passed since I had last seen Grandpa, and I had hoped to see him alive one more time so I could tell him goodbye, but now it was too late. Frustrated and sad, I called my mother and told her that I couldn't afford the trip then, and that I would have to come home later to visit the family.

After I talked with my mother, I sat down and tearfully remembered the good times that I had spent with Grandpa over many years. I said a prayer, and asked God to let me say goodbye to Grandpa in a dream, since I would not be at his funeral. After I said the prayer, I didn't think about it again.

Three days later, in the early morning hours on the day of Grandpa's funeral, I experienced what I can only describe as a "life-like" dream. Suddenly, I found myself standing on the side of a country road, and instantly knew that I was back home, and halfway between my parents' and grandparents' houses. It was summertime, and I stood there looking at trees with their green leaves that shimmered in the sunlight, and I was surprised that I could see fine details in the leaves in such a panoramic way.

While I was looking at the trees, a shiny black pickup truck came down the road toward me, and stopped to my right side. The passenger door opened, and to my amazement Grandpa stepped out. He was barely recognizable because he looked like he did in the prime of his life: he was much younger, his bald head had hair again, the deep scar on his upper lip that he had since childhood was now gone, and he stood at least a foot taller than I remembered.

Grandpa had a huge grin as he ran around his side of the truck toward me. I was very surprised to see him running because he had painfully suffered from an arthritic hip for forty years! I don't think that I ever saw him run in my life.

As I walked toward him, I noticed the round white stones on the ground. I could actually feel them crunching beneath my shoes! I remember thinking to myself, "This isn't real. This is just the dream that I wanted to have."

Grandpa held out his right hand to hold mine before giving me a hug, which was his customary way. Then I felt a very strong hand grasp mine and squeeze it hard. I felt heat radiating into my hand and up my arm to my elbow. As I gasped in disbelief, I actually felt the air going into my lungs.

Somehow, this really was my grandfather standing before me. I did not understand how this was possible, and yet it was. I quickly embraced Grandpa for a few seconds, and then he turned to leave.

I knew that he was on his way home, and he wanted to say good-bye before he left. As he climbed back into the truck, he reminded me of some things that I needed to do. I clearly heard his words in my mind without them being said.

Suddenly, the truck was gone, and I found myself back in my bed. I could still feel the blood rushing back into my hand as if it had just been squeezed. I was amazed by this experience and the memory of it firmly imprinted itself into my mind.

As I drove to work that morning, I was surprised by the absolute joy that I felt for my grandfather. It was impossible to be sad over his death anymore. He was happier than I had ever seen him before, and he was in better physical shape than I could have imagined. I felt humbled to have been given such an incredible experience, and wondered why it happened.

For several years after this, I couldn't get this experience out of my mind, and it would replay every so often. I wondered what I was supposed to do with this story. I knew that I was completely sure that there was life after death because I had held it in my own hand. It was beautiful, and from that moment, I never questioned it, because I knew it.

I had faith as a child, and was raised to believe in God, Jesus, and the afterlife; but when I actually felt my grandfather grasp my hand, I knew it was true. He made sure of it. That is why I wanted to share this story with all of you.

Over the years, I have told this story to several people who needed to hear it after they struggled with the loss of a loved one.

I noticed how it affected them, and helped to strengthen their faith. Now you know someone who has held the hand of a loved one after they passed into the afterlife. I hope that this story will renew your faith in God and Jesus.

CHAPTER 2

Four Rainbows

Several years before my grandfather's death, my husband and I wanted to start a family. We discovered that we had fertility problems, as some couples do when they are in their thirties. I was in my mid-thirties, and suddenly found out that I couldn't get pregnant. We met with the top infertility doctor in Atlanta. After some tests, he told us that we could begin infertility treatments at his clinic. After we learned what the treatments would cost, and that they were not covered by insurance, we thanked him for his time, and told him that we could not afford it. Our dream of having a family faded away.

As I approached the age of forty, the stress level regarding having a family increased dramatically. My 39th birthday was my worst one. Here I was, 39 years old with the man of my dreams, and I was not able to have the baby whom we both wanted so much. Ray and I had talked about having a family since we first knew each other. We never imagined that this would happen to us.

We simply did not have the money to deal with this situation. It seemed very unfair that insurance companies routinely exclude infertility treatments from their plans. All I knew was that if I were ever going to get pregnant, it had better happen soon.

We had saved money for a down payment on a house, and we could use that for one or two infertility treatments. I had to decide whether or not I was foolishly hanging on to our dream of becoming parents. The treatments would take all the money, and there were no guarantees that they would work, because the doctor had talked about a schedule of five or six treatment cycles, not just one or two.

I honestly did not know what to do. The sensible thing would be to use our money to buy a house, but my emotional side refused to give up my dream of becoming a mother. As the time went by, I wrestled with this decision unsuccessfully.

I finally gave up trying to make this decision, and decided to simply put it in God's hands. I said a prayer, told Him that I couldn't make the decision myself, and that I didn't know what the right path was; only He knew the right thing to do. I gave Him 100% control, asked Him to let me know His will, and that I would follow His decision on which path I was supposed to take. Afterwards, I felt a tremendous sense of relief, because I didn't have to carry this burden anymore.

Within a few weeks, I received my answer. As things turned out, it wasn't about which dream would claim our savings account. Amazingly, the decision was something that I had never even considered. God simply decided to cure me of my medical condition!

How impossible it all seemed after so many years of infertility that He would decide to cure me.

My medical condition was gone, and this reminded me of the Bible story where a woman came up behind Jesus and touched the edge of his cloak, and immediately her bleeding stopped, and she was healed. He felt His power go out to her, and she was cured because of her faith in Him. I believe that God decided to cure me because I finally decided to trust Him.

After six months went by, I still was not pregnant, and I started wondering if it was God's will for me to have a child. I said a prayer, and asked God for a sign that it would happen, and that I was not just imagining it.

Within two days, I had my answer. A thunderstorm had come through the city, and it stopped raining just as I walked outside the building into the parking lot to go home. I looked at my car, and above my car in the sky were *four rainbows!* One was very high, and the other three were below it. Of the three below, one was very bright, with two lighter rainbows underneath it. I had never seen anything like this in my life! Who had ever heard of a quadruple rainbow? I looked it up, and read that this was a very rare occurrence. The conditions have to be just right: dark thunderclouds, a heavy downpour, and the sun breaks through the clouds at the right moment.

Of course, the rainbows reminded me of the story about Noah's Ark, and the sign of the rainbow meant that God had promised mankind that He would never send another flood.

When I saw those four rainbows in the sky, I knew that God had just made a promise to me, and I knew He would keep it. I knew that I didn't have to worry, and I would be getting pregnant sometime soon.

A few months later, I had a dream: I was sitting in an office chair in an empty room in my building. In my lap sat a two-year-old little boy with wavy blond hair that tickled my chin as we rolled around the room. As I pushed myself from one side of the room to the other, he laughed with the sweetest little giggle.

The next morning, I told Ray that we were going to have a little boy who had wavy blond hair and the funniest little giggle. Of course, my husband had his doubts about this, but three months later I was pregnant! Exactly nine months later, I gave birth to a baby boy with blond hair who weighed eight pounds and 3 ounces. We named him Evan Michael Messick. It was just as God had promised me.

The next year, we were able to move into our first home using the money that we had not spent on infertility treatments. Our house was only a year and a half old, and was the color that I had always wanted: light gray siding with a dark roof and white trim.

God kept His promise to me. We had our child, and a new house. God generously gave us both of our dreams.

CHAPTER 3

A Parent's Worst Nightmare

After we had moved into our new house, we were happy that Evan was doing so well. He was a beautiful child, and also was really intelligent. He loved his books, and always enjoyed having us read to him. When he was only eighteen months old, he learned how to spell words using colorful block letters. Several months later, we started to notice that he was gradually losing interest in playing with the letters and his toys. He seemed distracted, and had not yet begun to talk.

At first, I wasn't too worried because one of my younger brothers did not start talking until he was almost three years old. We took Evan to our pediatrician for a check-up a week after his 2nd birthday, and told the doctor our concerns about Evan's lack of talking, and that he seemed to be distracted. The doctor gave Evan a very thorough exam which included the standard measurements of height and weight, but when he measured the circumference of Evan's head, he told us that it was slightly larger than it was supposed to be. Since Evan was not talking yet, the doctor made an appointment for Evan to have a CT scan to make sure that everything was normal.

We took Evan to the hospital for his CT scan, and the next day we picked up the films from the Radiology Office and took them to Dr. Andrew Reisner to find out the results. We learned that Evan had a cranial arachnoid cyst which was crushing one-third of the left side of his brain. That explained why Evan was unable to talk and had growing concentration problems. Evan needed an immediate operation to put in a shunt which would drain the excess fluid away from his brain.

We were stunned over the diagnosis, but quickly agreed to have Dr. Reisner perform the procedure. The surgery went well, and there were no complications. With the internal pressure gone, the left side of his brain expanded back to its normal size as much as it could. Evan would need speech therapy, and no one made any promises about how successful the outcome would be.

About six months later, another big problem had begun. Evan had gradually lost his appetite, and did not want to eat. I had to threaten him with turning off the television in order to get him to eat anything. We took him to our pediatrician about this new behavior, and were referred to several nutritionists who were unable to solve his eating problem. Evan continued to lose weight, and we were very worried.

In desperation, I told one of my associates about the situation. His wife worked for another pediatrician who was supposed to be excellent, so I immediately called and made an appointment. A few days later, Ray took Evan to see Dr. Judith R. Tolkan. She performed an exam, took a blood sample, and promised to call us with the results.

A few hours later, she called us and said that we should take Evan to the hospital for an immediate blood transfusion. When we arrived at the emergency room, the hospital staff started the transfusion and numerous other tests. An hour later, Dr. Bradley A. George told us that Evan had A.L.L., which is acute lymphoblastic leukemia.

This diagnosis really floored us, and we were in a state of shock. We were told that much progress had been made, and the survival rate had increased to about eighty-five percent. Of course, I was thinking about the fifteen percent that would not survive, and I worried that Evan might be in that group.

During the first week, I took some time off from work and stayed in the hospital with Evan. He had to have blood transfusions, spinal taps, and all types of tests. Then Evan began his chemotherapy protocol which would take three and a half years to complete.

I cried every night after Evan fell asleep in his hospital bed. I couldn't seem to stop crying, and went through many boxes of tissues. I was physically, emotionally, and spiritually drained. When I would wake up each morning, I would realize where I was and think, "Oh my God, my son has leukemia!"

I had waited for so long for this child, and didn't want to lose him to this disease. Now I understood what Abraham must have felt like when God asked him to give back his long-awaited only child. Abraham and his wife had also faced the problem of infertility, and didn't have a child until they were both very old. Then they had a miracle child whom they did not want to lose.

Abraham proved his faithfulness to God by agreeing to let God have his son back if that was His will. I know it must have broken Abraham's heart. He didn't know that God was only testing him to see if he would give up his only son because God had asked him. Abraham simply decided to trust God.

Now I had to trust God, too. I didn't want to lose my precious son either, but I had to be willing to give him back to God if that was what He wanted. I struggled with this for days until finally I told God that if it really was His will to take Evan back, then I would accept it. However, if He did take back my son, I asked that He would give me ten years with Evan first.

Asking for ten years is quite a lot to ask for when your child has leukemia, because tomorrow may be your child's last day. Chemotherapy reduces white blood cell counts to almost zero, and if your child develops a serious infection, he can die within a few hours. So, it was like asking for the moon when I asked for ten years; but as a mother, I asked for those years with Evan anyway.

CHAPTER 4

Live In Faith, Not In Fear

The first few weeks that Evan was treated for leukemia were a very chaotic and fearful time for us because we were so afraid that we would lose Evan to this disease. Fortunately, we had skilled doctors and nurses in a highly rated local children's hospital. They repeatedly told us that there were many years of research on treating leukemia, and that the success rates continued to rise every year.

There were five different chemotherapy protocols that could be used to treat Evan's leukemia. He was initially placed on the "standard" protocol, but it failed to produce the required level of remission. Evan was put on the strongest protocol, and it would take three and a half years to complete.

This treatment protocol required that Evan receive many different kinds of drugs on an ever-changing schedule. We had to learn how to give Evan some of those drugs at home when he was not in the clinic or the hospital. Kitchen cabinets that used to be filled with pots and pans were now filled with feeding tubes, feeding pump bags, cases of formula, boxes of plastic syringes, alcohol wipes, saline and heparin syringes, and various kinds of medicine. Because Evan was on the strongest protocol, he had to be fed the formula through a feeding tube. A food pump attached to a hospital pole stand became a permanent fixture in our great room, so that Evan could watch television while the food pump was operating.

The hospital became our second home. Ray took care of Evan in the hospital during the weekdays, and I would stay with Evan in the hospital on the weekends. We slept on a small sofa in his hospital room, and there was a bathroom with a toilet and shower. It was comforting to be surrounded by caring people who understood our struggle, and were willing to do anything to help Evan overcome this disease.

During the years of Evan's chemotherapy, we never drove more than one hour away from the Children's Healthcare of Atlanta at Scottish Rite hospital. We didn't go on vacations or take any long trips because it wasn't possible. We had to be able to get Evan to the emergency room any time he had a fever of 101 degrees or more, because this was the sign that he had just developed a serious infection.

I remember one frightening time when Evan developed a high fever and we went to the emergency room. The infection was very dangerous, Evan's blood pressure became very low, and his heart rate went over 180 beats per minute. Dr. Louis B. Rapkin gave Evan a large dose of antibiotics, and told my husband and me that, "The next 30 minutes will be critical." I stood next to Evan and held his hand. We looked at each other in silence, and waited for the antibiotics to work.

The antibiotics worked in time, but it was very close to disaster. The doctor said if we had arrived 30 minutes later, that Evan would not have survived. They took him upstairs to the Pediatric Intensive Care Unit for the night. We were very thankful to be able to take our son home again.

As Evan progressed through his chemotherapy protocol, there were many other dangerous times. Instead of the next 30 minutes being critical, we would be told that the next week would be critical, meaning that we could lose him at any time during that week. I had to put more and more faith in God because so much was out of our hands, and I had to struggle with danger almost every day. I lived with it through daily reminders of God's love for us.

I printed a series of Bible Scriptures, placed them on self-adhesive flexible magnets, and stuck them on the refrigerator. Every time I went to the refrigerator, I would see them and be reminded that I had to put my faith in God and trust Him each day. I wanted to share some of those Scriptures with you.

The first Scripture was from Luke 1:37, *For nothing will be impossible with God.* I had to believe that God could do anything. I had to trust that He could do the impossible, even for me personally.

Another Scripture that helped was from Philippians 4:13, *I can do all things through Christ who strengthens me.* These words helped me to get up every day and face the nightmare of my son having to go through chemotherapy.

From Matthew 17:20, Jesus said, *"If you have faith as small as a mustard seed...nothing will be impossible for you."* I knew that through faith in God, I could become strong enough to handle anything that came my way.

I took comfort in this Scripture from 1 John 5:14, *And this is the confidence we have toward Christ, that if we ask anything according to his will, he hears us.* I remember the many times I would pray that my son would be cured. Somehow Evan continued to find joy in his daily activities, and did his best to fight leukemia without letting it define him.

I felt strongly about the Scripture from Jeremiah 29:11, *For I know the plans I have for you, declares the Lord, plans for your welfare and not for evil, to give you a future and a hope.* This helped me believe that my son still had a future, and that God would always look out for him.

I continued to look at these and other Bible Scriptures every day, and remind myself of the possibilities. I began to understand that you are never in complete control of anything in your life. You must have faith in God, and be willing to give up control to Him. I got up every day, said my prayers, and put what I could not control in God's hands. I continued to believe that Evan could be cured, and I decided that I would live in faith, and not in fear.

CHAPTER 5

The Last Day

After about two years of chemotherapy, Evan's treatment protocol became less severe. We had celebrated his 5th birthday, and Ray and I had been discussing whether or not Evan would be able to attend school. After talking with his doctors, we decided to go for it. Ray met with an Assistant Director of Special Education for Forsyth County Schools, and they discussed having Evan enrolled in kindergarten class. Ray brought Evan to her office for an evaluation, and he was accepted into the Special Education program at Sharon Elementary School. Evan would attend Sharon Elementary for the 2003-2004, 2004-2005, and 2005-2006 school years. Evan loved going to school, and he loved his teachers. His chemotherapy was successfully finished in October 2004, and we hoped that everything would improve and stabilize.

During the summer of 2005, his blood counts began to fall, and Evan was diagnosed with relapsed leukemia in October 2005. This was very bad news because his chances of survival after a relapse were only fifty percent at best.

Evan had been on the strongest treatment path during his first treatment protocol—and it had failed. The chemotherapy protocol for his relapsed leukemia would be as severe as the doctors could make it.

We spent about three weeks a month in the clinic or the hospital for the next two years. The chemotherapy protocol was even worse than we expected. Evan's white blood cell counts did not rebound quickly, and he was frequently getting infections. We maintained a routine for Evan, and kept him occupied with his favorite books, DVDs, and his laptop computer. Therapists for physical, occupational, and speech therapy would come by several times a week and take him downstairs for an hour of fun. Kerri, Liz, and Terry were essential in keeping our spirits up, and Evan loved them. We also took walks on every floor of the hospital, the playground, and outside to the koi pond behind the hospital where we would count the colorful fish. Evan enjoyed walking outside in the fresh air and sunshine, and he was always happier afterwards. We were always careful with Evan on all of these walks, because his brain condition made him a little unsteady at times, and we didn't want him to trip and fall down.

Evan attended Shiloh Point for the 2006-2007 school year and transferred to Daves Creek Elementary for the 2007-2008 school year. He finished his chemotherapy protocol on May 9, 2008. We hoped for a summer with no problems.

If the treatment for relapsed leukemia fails to work, then the disease returns quickly. Evan was diagnosed again with relapsed leukemia on July 7, 2008. His birthday was six days later on July 13th, and we knew that it would be his last one. The ten years that I had asked for were over, and God was going to take him back.

Now we were out of options. We had a serious discussion with the doctors, and decided against experimental treatments that were not expected to work. Evan would be given regular chemotherapy in doses that he could tolerate. The goal was for Evan to return to school, and enjoy this time for as long as possible. We knew that eventually the drugs would fail, and have to be stopped.

At the beginning of the next school year, Ray had a meeting with the assistant principals and Evan's teachers, and told them that Evan had less than six months to live. Everyone was shocked, since Evan had done so well before the summer break, and his teachers started crying. Everyone agreed that they would help in any way possible.

Evan was able to attend school on a fairly regular basis, and made it to the Christmas break. We tried to have a normal Christmas morning and opened the presents together, but Evan was not feeling well, and he only smiled once. His health began to decline more quickly after Christmas, and he was not able to return to school again.

On February 3, 2009, I was very tired when I got up that morning. Evan had tossed and turned all night, which I had heard through the baby monitor. I had gone into his room several times to comfort him, and tell him to go back to sleep.

I called into work, and said that I would be late. I wanted to get Evan up for the morning, and have some time with him. He touched my hair, and gave me a big smile. It had been awhile since he had smiled at me, and I missed it. When I left for work, and let Ray take over, I gave Evan a hug and a kiss. I told him that I loved him, and would see him that night. That was the last time I saw him alive.

Late that afternoon, Ray called me at work, and said that Evan had passed away. He had been sitting on the great room sofa next to Ray, and was watching a favorite television show. The hospice nurse had stopped by a half hour earlier, and was also sitting on the sofa. Evan put his head down, as if to take a nap, and passed away. The nurse said his heart just stopped. When I heard this, it felt like my heart stopped too.

All of a sudden, I thought, "Oh no, he's really gone now!" Although I had over seven and a half years to prepare myself, I was still not ready when it happened. I told my supervisor, and immediately left the office. I desperately needed time off. I needed to deal with my new reality.

As I drove home that afternoon, I saw a beautiful sky, with the rays of the sun streaming down through the clouds. I felt very sad that I wasn't there when my son passed away, but if I had been, I don't know how I could have taken it.

When I arrived home, Evan was still sitting on the sofa, because the people from the funeral home had not yet come by to pick him up. He had a smile on his face; it was such a beautiful, sweet smile.

He looked happy, as if he could see something I couldn't see; I wondered what it could have been.

Then I remembered the times when he was a little boy, and I would rock him to sleep. We sat in a blue rocking chair with the ceiling light off, and the door to his room half open. I would sing the Christmas song, "Silent Night." It was like a lullaby. Evan just loved that song, and always smiled when I sang it. The words really do make it sound like a Heavenly lullaby.

There were several times that I remember him looking around my shoulder while I was rocking him to sleep. Evan would look up near the ceiling, smile, and wave his hand as if he saw something up there. I would turn around, and try to see what had his attention, but I never saw anything. Yet, he seemed to be fascinated, and looking as if someone was there, and looking down at him. I could sense that some connection I couldn't see was being made, and I could feel the hair on the back of my neck rise up.

I also remember several times when I put him down for a nap in a completely dark room. Later, I would hear Evan giggling and laughing loudly, and I would wonder what could possibly be so entertaining for him. Since he was not able to speak understandable English because of his brain condition, it was impossible for me to know why he was laughing. I just had to add it to the list of things that I didn't understand.

After Evan passed away, I started to make a connection with these incidents. I believe that Evan had seen his guardian angel, and since he didn't know any relatives who had died, his guardian angel was the one who came to take him home to Jesus. She must have been the one who made him smile again as he passed into the afterlife. I didn't have to worry that he had been alone; his guardian angel was with him.

After my son was taken away, I noticed how quiet it was. I actually heard the "tick tock tick tock" coming from the clock on the fireplace mantel. We had lived in this house for almost ten years, and I had never noticed it before. Now that Evan was gone, I heard it, and the silence seemed deafening in a strange way.

Many months later, I realized how God must have felt when Jesus died on the cross. I believe that God did not want to see His Son die, but allowed it to happen for the sake of our salvation. It must have been very hard, as it was for me. We both had to let our sons go.

One day, this will all seem to pass as quickly as a blink of an eye, and I will be with Evan again. I know that God truly understood what I went through that day. He just wanted to tell me, "*Don't worry about Evan. I'll take over from here.*"

CHAPTER 6

The Memorial Service

One problem we had to face immediately after our son passed away was where to have his memorial service. We used to go to church every Sunday before Evan was born, but once he developed leukemia, that was no longer possible. In the meantime, we had moved to our new house, which was far north from Peachtree Presbyterian Church in Atlanta.

My husband and I looked on the internet for churches in our area, made a list, and drove by each one to help us decide. One of the churches was Alpharetta Presbyterian Church, and we made an appointment to see inside the church and meet the pastors.

When we walked into the sanctuary, I immediately knew this was the right place, because it had a huge stained-glass rose window on the wall in front. I loved rose windows, and collected photographs of them. This one was colorful, simple in design, and illustrated important stories in the Bible.

I looked up at the right side of the sanctuary, and saw another round stained-glass window. The image showed the sun streaming through the clouds, like a stairway to Heaven. The window looked just like the sky on the day that Evan passed away. This was where I wanted his memorial service.

We met with the Senior Pastor, Dr. G. Oliver Wagner, and his Associate Pastor, and told them that we used to attend Peachtree Presbyterian before Evan was born, that he had developed leukemia, and recently passed away. We needed a church for his memorial service, and wanted it close to home. The pastors agreed to let us have the church for Evan's service. They told us that they were fairly new to this church, and that this would be the first memorial service since they had arrived.

As Ray and I made the arrangements, we discussed Evan's eulogy. I told Ray that I wanted to write it, and he agreed. I asked Dr. Wagner if he would read the Scripture readings and the eulogy for me during the service, because I could not without crying, and he agreed. Dr. Wagner and his Associate Pastor also agreed to read seventeen letters that we had received from Evan's nurses, teachers, and therapists.

The sunlight streamed in through the rose window on the day of Evan's memorial service. We all sang the great hymn, "Amazing Grace." Ray and I had chosen two readings from the New Testament. The first reading was Mark 10:13-16, *They were bringing children to him that he might touch them, and the disciples rebuked them. But when Jesus saw it, he was indignant and said to them, "Let the children come to me; do not hinder them, for to such belongs the kingdom of God. Truly, I say to you, whoever does not receive the kingdom of God like a little child shall not enter it." And he took them in his arms and blessed them, laying his hands on them.*

The second Bible reading was from Romans 8:35, 37-39, *Who shall separate us from the love of Christ? Shall trouble, or distress, or persecution, or famine, or nakedness, or danger, or sword? No, in all these things we are more than conquerors through him who loved us. For I am sure that neither death nor life, nor angels nor rulers, nor things present nor things to come, nor powers, nor height nor depth, nor anything else in all creation, will be able to separate us from the love of God in Christ Jesus our Lord.*

After the readings, Dr. Wagner read the eulogy, and then he and his Associate Pastor took turns reading the seventeen letters. I heard so many good things said about Evan that day. He truly was an inspiration to so many of us.

After all the letters were read aloud, Ray's cousin, Linda, a talented musician, sang a song from her compact disc. The name of the song was, "When the Night is Falling" by Dennis Jernigan, and Linda played her acoustic guitar as she sang. After that, Linda played and sang, "Silent Night." I think that everyone who heard the eulogy and that song will remember Evan, and that I sang "Silent Night" to him every night at his bedtime.

After the service ended, everyone went outside. Ray had ordered some white dove-shaped paper balloons from Ecolovy Balloon LLC in Japan. They were the same balloons that were used in the opening ceremony for the 1998 Winter Olympics in Nagano, Japan. Ray filled the ten balloons with helium, and we released them into the sky: ten balloons for the ten years that we had Evan in our lives.

Before the memorial service began, the sound technician for the church had set up a stereo system on the outdoor patio next to the area where the balloons would be released. As the balloons rose into the sky, the song, "Better Days Ahead" by Norman Brown, was played. This song was Evan's favorite piece of music: an instrumental solo that was cheerful, expressive, very upbeat, and performed by a genius guitarist.

This song was on a CD that had been in my car's player for years. It was the second song on the CD, so every time that I took Evan somewhere in my car, he would immediately lean forward from the back seat, and hold up two fingers that meant, "Mom, play the second song again."

It was fitting to have this music playing as we watched the ten white balloons rise into a clear blue sky. We were letting go of our son; giving him back to God. We had not lost him forever, because we knew that he was in Heaven. We would never see the balloons again, but one day, we will see Evan again. Until then, we will always remember and honor him.

CHAPTER 7

You're Not
The Only One

I remember the first time when one of my friends died. She was only twenty years old, and I had known her since grade school. She was Irish, had so much vitality, and was a great person. My friend died in an avalanche while skiing in the Rocky Mountains. Until that tragedy, my experiences with death were limited to elderly people.

My friend's mother was an English teacher who had taught me in the sixth grade. She was devastated by her daughter's death. Her bubbly spirit was completely crushed, and every time I saw her, she had a grief-stricken look on her face. She had other children, but she still withdrew from life.

I had a cousin who died in a car accident when she was only twenty years old. In earlier times, I was her occasional babysitter. We spent holidays together with our grandparents and other relatives. I took her high school senior photographs, and was there to celebrate with her when she graduated. I never thought we would lose her at such a young age. She was supposed to have her whole life in front of her, and then she was gone. My aunt had a very difficult time dealing with the tragic loss of her daughter, and visited the cemetery every day for many years.

One of my co-workers lost his beautiful daughter to a disease when she was only four years old. They were not able to deal with this tragedy, and their marriage ended in divorce. The statistics show that there is a 75% chance of divorce if a child has a life-threatening disease, or if the child dies.

I remember my younger sister calling me periodically to ask how Ray and I were doing. Laura is a pathologist, and she looks at slides with a microscope, and writes the reports that say whether or not someone has cancer. I knew she was a little afraid that the awful strain of Evan's leukemia and death would cause serious problems for my marriage.

After Evan died, many people told me that if their child ever died, then they would just die too. I understood how they could say that, but you can't let the death of your child destroy everything else in your life. You still have a spouse, other children, family, and friends who need you.

You must have faith that your child went to Heaven. Because I held my grandfather's hand soon after he had passed away, I knew that there really is a place called Heaven. It is a physical place, and not an imaginary place up in the clouds.

From John 14:1-3, Jesus said, *"Let not your hearts be troubled. Believe in God; believe also in me. In my Father's house are many rooms. If it were not so, would I have told you that I go to prepare a place for you? And if I go and prepare a place for you, I will come again and will take you to myself, that where I am you may be also."*

People in Heaven are happy to be there. I was happy for my grandfather, because he was joyous and at peace. If things worked out so well for him, why wouldn't they also work out for my son? Evan was a wonderful child, and I know that Jesus loves him. I know that Evan's physical limitations have been healed. God restores us and makes everything new again.

From Revelation 21:4, *He will wipe away every tear from their eyes, and death shall be no more, neither shall there be mourning, nor crying, nor pain anymore, for the former things have passed away.*

After Evan died, I made the decision that I was not going to be destroyed by losing him. If I had a choice, I would rather go and be with him there, instead of bringing him back here. I don't feel as connected to my life here anymore, because now I have a child in Heaven. I look forward to the day when I will see my child again, and so should you.

CHAPTER 8

The Guilt Trip

Once I had a conversation with a friend about religion, and I told her the story about seeing my grandfather after he had passed away. I described how he held my hand, how I could actually feel the strength and warmth of his hand squeezing mine, and his incredible sense of peace and joy.

When I finished my story, she told me that she had always felt a special connection to God. Sometimes she would have thoughts come into her mind about people or situations, and later the situation would happen in such a way that she could make a difference.

Then she told me about something that had distressed her for many years. One day her teenage cousin started having a lot of pain, and he was taken to the hospital for some tests. She had gone to the hospital to be with the family, and while she waited with them, the thought came into her mind that her cousin had a kidney problem.

When the doctor met with the family to discuss the tests that he was ordering, she did not ask the doctor if this might be a kidney problem. Because of the confusion and drama, she also did not tell her family members about her thought that it was a kidney problem.

A few days later, she learned that her cousin had died in the hospital. After the autopsy, the family was told that a kidney problem was the cause of his death. After hearing this, she felt incredible guilt for not having said anything when she had the chance. Every day, she felt the weight of guilt pressing down on her, and every family gathering was a reminder of her cousin who was gone. She no longer enjoyed her life.

She told me that after hearing my story about my grandfather, she began to feel the burden of guilt being lifted from her shoulders. She was finally able to believe that her cousin was now in Heaven. Now she could thank God that her cousin was in the place where there is only peace and love.

Sometimes circumstances surrounding the death of a child can fill your mind with unbearable guilt and sorrow. You can torture yourself with thoughts about what might have been done differently, if only you had known what to do. When a child dies, the parents will certainly grieve over the loss. Once the initial shock is over, however, our faith can help us realize that our loss is temporary, and not permanent.

We believe that Evan has moved on to a place of eternal happiness, and is now experiencing the wonderful things that God has planned especially for him. People in Heaven are protected by the angels, and join in the chorus of the saints. They live in harmony;

their new life is beyond our wildest imagination, and they are waiting for us to join them.

Jesus knew that we could not live successfully on the earth or in Heaven if we were burdened with sin and guilt. He died for us willingly, so that our sins could be forgiven. In John 10:11,18, Jesus said, "*I am the good shepherd. The good shepherd lays down his life for the sheep. No one takes it from me, but I lay it down of my own accord. I have authority to lay it down, and I have authority to take it up again. This charge I have received from my Father.*"

We need to accept the gift of salvation from our Lord and Savior, so that one day we can live in Heaven with Jesus, our children, our family, and our friends. In the meantime, we can live with gratitude, and follow His path for us.

CHAPTER 9

Honoring Traditions

The first year after Evan died was the most difficult year of my life. I remembered the family traditions and holidays that we had shared: Easter, Mother's Day, my birthday, Father's Day, Evan's birthday, Thanksgiving, Ray's birthday, and Christmas. I didn't want to face those special days without Evan. I didn't fully realize the impact of his absence until he wasn't there anymore. It felt like there was a hole in my heart that could never be healed in my lifetime.

Evan's birthday was on July 13th. A week before his birthday, Ray and I ordered a beautiful bouquet of red and white flowers which were placed in the church sanctuary on Sunday, in remembrance of Evan. We never discussed his birthday on the actual day; it was too painful to talk about.

As Christmas drew closer that first year, I really didn't want to decorate the house, and put up the Christmas tree if Evan wasn't going to be sitting next to it. After thinking about it for a while, I remembered just how much Evan loved the Christmas season. We had miniature white lights placed all around the great room, on the bushes outside the great room windows, and around the windows. Our Christmas tree had multi-colored lights, an assortment of ornaments that we had collected over the years, and Evan's bright green and red train set that circled the tree.

A colorful ceramic nativity set was placed on top of my piano to remind us of the humble place where Jesus was born. On the fireplace mantel, we had a ceramic church, a gazebo, and a town square of nineteenth-century-era people singing Christmas carols, playing in the snow, and riding in a horse-drawn carriage. A large wreath from our first Christmas together as a married couple was on the wall in the foyer.

I remembered how Evan wanted all the Christmas lights turned on every morning as soon as he walked into the room. Every night after I came home from work, I would take him on a drive around the neighborhoods so he could look at all of the Christmas displays. I played Christmas music on the radio as we drove around, and we had a great time together.

I decided that it just wouldn't be Christmas if I didn't honor our family tradition of putting up our Christmas tree that year. I needed to turn on all those lights again in memory of all the happy times we had spent with Evan. I wanted him to look down from Heaven and smile when he saw the lights.

We celebrated that first Christmas without Evan as best we could, and we remembered him every Christmas after that by putting up all the decorations, and looking at our pictures of the three of us together.

As the birthdays and holidays came around every year, we continued to honor Evan by having flowers in the church on his birthday. We did not avoid those special days; instead, we did something special together that Evan would have enjoyed doing with us. In that way, we remembered him, and continued our family traditions so he can live on in our hearts.

One thing that Ray does for me on Mother's Day and my birthday is to give me a beautiful card that he signs from Evan. Ray does this because if my son were here, he would have given me the cards. The cards remind me that I am still a parent. The location of my child is not the determining factor. Just because Evan isn't here with me doesn't mean that I am no longer a mother; I still am.

Always remember your child loved you, and still does. Your sadness will subside over time if you allow it to do so. You have to think of your child in a different way. He or she has moved on to another place where you haven't been yet. Believe in God, and remember that one day you will be with your child again. Continue to remember your child's life by honoring the traditions that you shared together.

CHAPTER 10

Watching Over Us

W hen people pass into the afterlife, I believe there are times when they are allowed to communicate with us, if it serves God's purposes.

The first time that I heard a story about this was from a friend who had lost both of her parents. Her mother had died when she was four years old, and her father died a year later. Her only remaining family was an aunt who was single, and not ready to take on the responsibility of raising her five-year-old niece; and so, her aunt placed her into an orphanage.

As you know, most people who want to adopt children prefer babies, so they can raise them as if they were biological children. The older the child, the more difficult it is to be adopted, and my friend came to this realization very quickly.

On her first Christmas in the orphanage, my friend was very

sad because both of her parents were gone, and nobody wanted to adopt her. She felt that her life was already over. Later that day, she told me that her mother appeared to her in her room, and told her to not be sad and not to worry, because very soon a family would come to the orphanage and they would adopt her. Her mother told her the last name of the family, and said that they were the right family for her. My friend remembered being very happy because everything wasn't hopeless after all.

The next day, a family arrived at the orphanage and asked if there were any little girls around five years old. These parents had brought their only child: a girl who was five years old. The parents were not able to have more children, and wanted their daughter to have a sister.

The administrator of the orphanage brought my friend in to meet the family, and introduced them. The family had the *same last name* that my friend's mother had said was the right family for her! The family soon adopted her and took her home. Now she was part of a new family who would love her.

I remember the time when one of my uncles lost his wife to cancer. They had started dating as young teenagers, had been together for over thirty years, and married for over twenty-five years. She was the light of his life, and they had one daughter. My aunt was a wonderful person who was attractive, funny, intelligent, and loved animals, especially horses. After she was diagnosed with cancer, my uncle bought her a horse, and she rode the horse until her health failed.

After she died, my uncle became very depressed. He tried to resume his life, but still grieved deeply over losing her. Loneliness drove him to try dating again, but no one could replace the woman he had loved for so many years.

My uncle started marking out the day she died on each month of the calendar on the wall. He refused to go to work on that day every month. He stayed at home and started drinking while he grieved, and this continued for months.

One night, he woke up after midnight, when a bright light appeared on one side of the bedroom. His wife stood there talking with two other people whom he didn't know. She was young again, beautiful, and happy. He couldn't understand what they were saying, but it must have been funny, because they were laughing. He was simply amazed to see her there.

Knowing my aunt, I think she was allowed to briefly come back to let her husband see that she was having a wonderful time, and that he should be happy for her. This was a huge turning point for my uncle, and he was then able to find peace. He moved past his grief, and started living his life again.

I remember the time when my brother Dennis became very sick with the flu. Dennis and his wife, Kim, had a baby girl who was almost one year old. Kim was staying at home and taking care of Katie full time. Dennis had a high fever as one of his symptoms, was sleeping on and off during the day, and Kim was checking on him throughout the day.

While Dennis was lying in his bed, he noticed two men standing at the foot of the bed. He had never seen them before, and had no idea who they were. They were just talking softly with each other, and looked over at him from time to time.

My brother fell asleep again, and when he woke up, these men were still there in his room. When Kim came back in to check on Dennis, he asked her, "Who are these men in my room, and why are they here?" Kim told Dennis that he was hallucinating, because there was no one else in the room.

Dennis didn't understand why Kim couldn't see them, and said, "They're standing right there at the end of the bed!" Kim dismissed his remark, left the room to check on Katie, and one of the men said to the other one, "He's going to be all right now." Then they were suddenly gone.

A month later, Dennis was visiting our Aunt Theresa. She was showing him some old family photo albums. He had not seen one of the old albums before, and as they looked through it, he saw a picture of the two men who had been in his room!

Dennis quickly asked my aunt, "Who are the two men in this picture?" She said, "That man is your Grandfather Louis, and the other man is your Great Grandfather Frank." My brother was absolutely amazed and told her, "They are the two men who were in my room that day when I was really sick. They were standing there, and talking to each other!"

My aunt quickly made the sign of the cross when she heard this. Great Grandfather Frank had died years before Dennis was born, and Grandfather Louis had died when Dennis was only three years old. Dennis had no idea who the men were until that moment, and then he knew the truth: his great grandfather and grandfather had been watching over him while he was very sick!

As time passed, Dennis and Kim had four more children, and all of them were sons: Dean, Derek, Dylan, and Dustin. My other two brothers never had any sons. Our family name would continue because those four children were born; our grandfathers had made sure of that. Dennis has nine grandchildren, with the possibility of more in the future.

We need to realize that our loved ones who have passed away have not stopped loving us. In Heaven, they have a greater capacity to love us, because they are in God's presence.

One of my favorite Scriptures is 1 Corinthians 13:4-8, 13, *Love is patient and kind; love does not envy or boast; it is not arrogant or rude. It does not insist on its own way; it is not irritable or resentful; it does not rejoice at wrongdoing, but rejoices with the truth. Love bears all things, believes all things, hopes all things, endures all things. Love never ends. So now faith, hope, and love abide, these three; but the greatest of these is love.*

CHAPTER 11

Why Am I Still Here?

I have had several different occurrences in my life that really made me wonder why I'm still here. I don't know why God has saved some people, but not others. I wanted to know why things happened the way they did, and know what God's plan was for my life.

In the summer of 1977, when I was twenty-one years old, my Uncle Owen invited me and my younger sister Laura to travel to Beaver Island, Michigan for a family vacation. Aunt Marie was pregnant with their fourth child, and decided to stay home. Uncle Owen brought their three other children who were eight years old or younger: Kathy, Joe, and Larry.

We drove to Charlevoix, took the ferry over to the island, and stayed in their log cabin. The construction of the cabin was rustic and used log beams. The bedrooms had walls, but did not have ceilings, and were open to the cabin's vaulted ceiling.

On Saturday night after supper, I put my young cousins to bed, and Uncle Owen went to sleep out on the porch which had a door that separated it from the inside of the cabin. Laura, who was twelve, went to sleep in the other bedroom.

As I was getting ready for bed, while brushing my teeth, suddenly a thought popped into my head: "*Open the window if you want to see the sun rise!*" I don't know why I had this thought. I didn't want to have the window open all night, because it was cold outside at night, even in the middle of the summer. I immediately put that thought out of my head.

In a flash, that thought was right back in my head again: "*Open the window if you want to see the sun rise!*" I ignored it as I combed the snarls out of my hair. Soon it was right back in my head again, only this time it was much more insistent; but I wasn't going to open that window. I went into the bedroom, closed the door, and got into the bed with Laura. Now the thought was repeating itself over and over: "*Open the window if you want to see the sun rise!*" I thought that I must be losing my mind.

Finally, I gave up. I got out of bed and opened both of the windows all the way. I felt a huge sense of relief. Laura said, "Why did you open the windows? It will get too cold in here." I said, "I'm sleeping with the windows open tonight. If you don't like that, then go sleep with Kathy in the other room." Laura left to sleep with Kathy, and I climbed back into bed. Since I was tired, I fell asleep almost immediately, and didn't wake up again until the next morning.

When I woke up, there was a terrible smell in the cabin. Everyone else was already in the kitchen, and eating cereal at the table. I went into the kitchen, and they complained loudly about the smell. I told them to be quiet, and I walked over to the gas stove. I heard a hissing sound coming from the stove, but none of the burners on top of the stove were turned on, so I opened the oven door and found the problem. The pilot light had gone out, and the control knob for the oven was pushed in. The stove had leaked gas into the entire cabin, because all the rooms were open to the vaulted ceiling.

I told everyone to get out of the cabin. A few minutes later, my uncle drove up the driveway. He had left the cabin from the porch earlier that morning, and had gone into town to have breakfast. He was not aware of the gas problem in the cabin, because the porch was screened and open to fresh air.

I told my uncle what had happened, and he helped me open all the windows and doors so the gas would escape from the cabin. This had been a deadly close call for us, and my uncle knew it. He asked me not to mention this to my Aunt Marie, because he knew that she would be very upset with him. I waited almost thirty years before I told her, which was about ten years after Uncle Owen had passed away.

Later that Sunday morning we went to church, and while we were there, I thought about what had almost happened to us, and the warnings I had received: *"Open the window if you want to see the sun rise!"* It must have been my guardian angel warning me. Thank goodness I finally listened to that message even though I didn't understand it at the time. I said a prayer of thanks, and have never forgotten what almost happened.

I often wondered why we had been spared; then I looked at what each of us had done with our lives. I became an operations manager in the mortgage industry. Laura became a pathologist. My cousins became a dental hygienist, a police officer, and a school teacher. We all had careers that helped people in various ways. Somehow, I wasn't surprised after all.

Another incident occurred about two years after Ray and I were married. We were living in Atlanta in an apartment which was located on Cobb Parkway, and south of the Galleria Mall. Cobb Parkway has heavy traffic, so there is a traffic light at the entrance of the apartment complex. My office was south of the complex, so I had to make a left turn onto Cobb Parkway when driving to work.

One morning I was the first car in line waiting for the traffic light to turn green. I remember a voice in my head that asked, *"Are you really in that much of a hurry to get to work today?"* I thought to myself, "No, I guess I'm not in that much of a hurry to get to work today."

Instead of zooming out as soon as the light turned green, I hesitated for a few seconds. Just before I reached the middle of the intersection, a car ran through the red light and flew by the front of my car going at least fifty miles an hour! Wow, he just missed me by about two feet! I was quite shaken, but managed to calm down by the time that I got to my office.

A few minutes after I sat down at my desk, my older sister Mary

Ann called me on my business phone. She sounded rather strange, and asked me if I was okay. I told her that I was fine, and wanted to know why she was calling me at work early in the morning. She told me that she had a bad dream about me being in a horrible car accident. She dreamed that my car was hit on my door in the middle of an intersection, and I was killed instantly. But her dream had four parts: in the first part, I was killed; in the second part, the other car barely missed me; in the third part, I was killed; and in the fourth part, the other car barely missed me. Mary Ann said that her dream was so real that she had to call me to reassure herself that my car crash had not really happened.

Her four-part dream shocked me, and I told her, "As a matter of fact, I almost did get killed this morning!" Then I proceeded to tell her the whole story. We finally concluded that it must have been our guardian angels working overtime. Mary Ann's guardian angel was warning her about what could happen to me, and mine was trying to delay me so that the other car crashing into my car would not actually happen.

I cannot explain why God would want to spare me again. I know that it would have devastated my husband and family. I don't know why some people are spared and others are not.

I just felt thankful to be alive. In my heart, I knew that God wanted me to do something important with my life; otherwise, why would He bother? I just didn't know what it was. I wondered about it for years.

After my son Evan died, I finally came to realize that God wanted me to encourage people to have more faith in Him. There is so much tragedy in the world, but nothing can be compared to the death of your own child. You realize that people matter most in this world. We can lose our job, our house, and all our possessions, but we can work and replace them in time. We cannot replace our loved ones.

CHAPTER 12

Amazing Grace

In the Book of Job, we are told that Job was an upright, good man who feared God, and turned away from evil. He had seven sons, three daughters, thousands of sheep, camels, oxen, donkeys, and many servants. One day Satan challenged God and said that if Job had his family and possessions taken away, then Job would curse God and abandon his faith. God did not believe this, and allowed Job to be tested with losing everything. In just one day, the oxen and donkeys were stolen, the sheep and servants were killed, the camels were stolen, and a windstorm destroyed a family home with all Job's children inside the house, and none survived. From Job 1:21, he said, *"Naked I came from my mother's womb, and naked shall I return. The Lord gave, and the Lord has taken away; blessed be the name of the Lord."* And Satan returned with a second challenge for God, and said that if God also allowed Job to be tested with the loss of his health, then Job would curse God and abandon his faith. God then allowed Satan to inflict this second test upon Job, and he developed painful sores that covered his entire body. When this happened, from Job 2:9, Job's wife said, *"Do you still hold fast your integrity? Curse God and die."* Job's friends came to see him, but offered no true consolation, and made him feel worse by what they said. Job questioned why God would allow these things to happen to him. In spite of everything, he never lost his faith in God.

God saw that Job had remained faithful throughout his ordeal. God had been right about Job's character and faith. From Job 42:10, *"And the Lord restored the fortunes of Job, when he had prayed for his friends. And the Lord gave Job twice as much as he had before."* The numbers of his sheep, camels, oxen, and donkeys were doubled, and he had more children: seven sons and three daughters were his once again.

We have all had our share of trials in life with our jobs, finances, health, and trying to raise our children. But I will say that the death of my child was the most devastating thing that I have ever faced. Time itself is now measured by how long it will be before I can see Evan again.

Just like Job, I think that I've been in a battle for my soul since the day I was born. It's a struggle over whether or not I have faith in God and believe in His son, Jesus. I can either let the troubles of this world overwhelm and destroy me, or I can choose to believe that God will make things right in the end.

I have chosen to trust God in all things, and to have faith in the One who controls the universe and the happiness of my heart.

I may not understand why things happen, but I can accept them because I know that everything in this world is temporary. I have set my eyes on everlasting things instead.

I don't have to worry about tomorrow because Jesus specifically told us not to worry about it. From Matthew 6:25, *"Therefore I tell you, do not be anxious about your life..."* Jesus has gone ahead to prepare a place for us, just like he already did for Evan. I'm grateful for knowing that. His Grace is truly amazing.

CHAPTER 13

One Step Closer to Heaven

About two years after Evan passed away, I was diagnosed with Stage 4 breast cancer. Suddenly, I was in the same situation as my son had been—and I found it hard to believe. Now I was thinking that I would be seeing Evan much sooner than expected, and I discovered that I wasn't ready to go yet. I still had my list of things to do, and one of those things was writing this book. I have felt compelled to write it ever since I held my grandfather's hand in mine after he died.

Being diagnosed with Stage 4 breast cancer gave me a whole new perspective on time. I already knew that my time on earth is limited, but now all I want is more time. I don't know why my son died when he was ten, and I don't know why my time is much shorter than I expected. I did not realize how much I didn't want to die until my cancer diagnosis.

There were plans I had put on hold because I didn't feel like doing them. Perhaps it was the sadness that I felt after my son died, or maybe I just wasn't motivated enough back then. Getting breast cancer gave me the reason to finish the things that I really wanted to do, since I no longer had time to waste.

It is important to me to share with parents the fact that your child is not lost. One day, you will be together again with your child, and you will hear all the things that he or she has been doing. One day, I will be with Evan, and he will be able to speak to me with his own words; it will be our first time that we have a real conversation. I'll ask him, "What have you been doing during the last few years?" I can't wait to hear what he has to say! I also want to hear him tell me that he loves me. It's what every mother wants to hear; I just haven't heard him say it yet because of his brain condition that kept him from speaking understandable English.

In the meantime, I have things that I want to do, and I'm going to do them. I'm not going to waste the time I have left feeling sorry for myself. Being on the edge of death motivates me to want to live again.

You need to start living again, too. You need to decide what you want to do with the rest of your life. There are many things that you can do for other people, especially those who are hurting. You can listen to them, and give them the chance to talk about the child whom they have lost. You will find that they will tell you funny stories about their child, and they will start to smile again.

It's important to remember the stories about our children, and to tell others about them. Leave their pictures out on the fireplace mantel, the walls of the family room, and of course, on the refrigerator. Be thankful for the gift of your child, their influence on your life, and everything they meant to you.

You were privileged to bring your child into this world, and you can look forward to spending eternity with them. When you see your child again, it will be wonderful and full of joy! In the meantime, pray for wisdom, and keep your faith.

CHAPTER 14

Go to the Mountaintop

When I was in my mid-twenties, I went on a group tour to British Columbia. The most awe-inspiring thing we did was taking a helicopter ride over the nearby mountains. We flew to the top of a mountain, the helicopter would land, and we would get out, walk around, and take pictures of the rivers and valleys below us. On several mountains, we were higher than the clouds around us. On one mountain, I saw an eagle soaring high above us, and heard its piercing cry before it disappeared into the valley below. There was a sparkling blue lake below me that reflected the color of the sky. I took lots of pictures so I could capture those moments in time and never forget them. It was truly Heavenly while being up there. During that afternoon, I more clearly understood the Bible verse from Psalm 46:10, *"Be still, and know that I am God."*

Being up that high yielded a different perspective because

everything seemed so far away: no troubles or worries—just peace, serenity, and beautiful land that stretched out as far as the horizon.

When something happens that truly threatens to tear you apart, go to the mountaintop, if only in your mind, find your own special place of peace, and reach out to God in prayer. You don't have to understand everything; that's what it means to be still and know that God is the Alpha and the Omega, the Beginning and the End. Give Him your troubles, and let Him be your guide. From Hebrews 13:5, "*I will never leave you nor forsake you.*" From Matthew 28:20, "*And behold, I am with you always, to the end of the age.*"

God sent His beloved Son, Jesus, to be born into this world, to teach anyone willing to listen, and to ultimately die on our behalf so that we could be with Him and our family in Heaven forever.

CHAPTER 15

The Final Analysis

After losing my only son, Evan, I have come to some basic realizations about life and the afterlife which I want to share with you:

- God is always in control, no matter how it may seem.

- Miracles still happen, even if they are inexplicable.

- Never underestimate the power and mercy of God.

- No one is exempt from the trials of this world.

- If you trust God with small things, then you can have faith to trust Him with the big things, too.

- Nothing can separate us from the love of God.

- Live your life in faith, and not in fear.

- Honor and remember your loved one.

- No one is lost if you know where they are.

- You are still a parent, even if your child is not with you.

- Follow the example of Jesus by helping others in need.

- Life is a gift, so be sure to open it.

It is not The End, it's just

The Beginning

CHAPTER 16

No Bungee Jumping Allowed

The pilot of our small plane revved the engine for take-off, and conversation became impossible because the plane's cabin door was missing. Engine noise and air turbulence flooded the cabin as the plane left the ground. I looked down at the altimeter on my safety harness and watched the needle slowly rise to indicate 3,500 feet. I felt Donna's hand squeeze my arm. She was jumping first, and it was almost time for her to go. I remember thinking to myself, "How many people go skydiving on their third date?"

Donna and I were attending Georgia Southern University. A mutual friend had introduced us in the main cafeteria four weeks earlier. On the Monday following our second date, a skydiving company had set up a display booth in the cafeteria. Donna and I had seen the videos of people skydiving, but we had not discussed them, because neither of us had decided if we were actually going to jump. I had always told myself that skydiving was something that I wanted to try one day. But now, that day had unexpectedly arrived. Was I going to jump? I thought, "If that parachute doesn't open, that's a whole lot of studying down the drain!" On Thursday night, I decided that I was going to jump. I called Donna to tell her about it, and to ask her to go with me so she could take some pictures of me coming down. As soon as she heard my voice, she said, "Guess what I'm going to do? I'm going skydiving!" I said, "What are you talking about? I'm calling you to tell you that I'm going skydiving!" And so, we decided to have a skydiving date. We left the campus the next afternoon to go home, see our families— maybe for the last time?!— and to ask for the money to cover the cost of the class instruction and the jump. Of course, both sets of our parents told us that we were *"Absolutely Not Allowed"* to ever go skydiving. We returned to the University campus with no new money, but we had enough money saved from our summer jobs anyway, and so *We Were Going Skydiving!*

On Monday afternoon, we called and made our reservations for Saturday morning. We told our friends about our weekend plans, and were amused at the wide range of reactions that we received. On Saturday morning, Donna and I rode together in my car, while one of her friends followed us in another car; she would take the pictures as we came down. Upon arrival, we were introduced to the only other person who had decided to jump: another Georgia Southern student named Pete, who was also on the gymnastics team. We were given four hours of classroom instruction, and I learned important facts like, "Streamers have a high rate of descent." A streamer is what happens when the parachute does not open completely, and just flaps like a flag in a strong wind. Yikes! We took our lunch break, and then went outside to a wooden platform where we jumped off into the dirt over and over to practice landing. We put on the equipment, got into the plane, and talked until the engine was started.

As the plane flew into position over the landing zone, the jumpmaster gave us the ready signal. Donna moved into position under the plane's wing, and waited for the go signal. At the signal, Donna pushed away from the plane and arched her back. As she fell, the static line pulled her parachute out, and it opened perfectly. What a relief! Then it was my turn. I climbed out under the wing, waited for the signal, and pushed away. My parachute opened perfectly, and then I noticed that there was no sound at 3,000 feet. No one had mentioned this in class. I was moving at the same speed as the wind, so there was no wind noise. I was far above the ground, and could not hear any sounds from below. It was like floating back down to earth from outer space—simply amazing!

I pulled my lines, and steered the parachute to the landing zone, but by the time I was ready to land, the wind had picked up a little too much. I hit the ground going too fast, and was flipped from the impact. I stood up and waved that I was OK.

As I walked back from the landing zone, I looked up and watched as Pete was floating down. We took more pictures, and then drove back to the University campus.

Donna and I went to a party on the following Thursday night. The party was boring, so we did not stay out very late. We had talked about our adventure during the week, so we did not mention it again at the party. I thought that going skydiving together would have made us a stronger couple, but it was as if we had done too many important things too fast. In the movies, the couple that successfully meets a dangerous challenge always finds romance, but it did not work that way for us. We did not go out on another date after that. Maybe we should have battled aliens or zombies instead of going skydiving, but I don't remember them being very popular at that time. It seems that skydiving, aliens, zombies, and dating all have inherent risks. The lesson is clear: Taking great risks may yield great rewards, but success is never guaranteed.

Eleven years after my skydiving adventure, I saw another activity that looked like big fun: bungee jumping! I turned on the local news one night, and watched a report that a new company in Atlanta was building towers for bungee jumping. Somehow, I had never even heard of bungee jumping. I wrote down the name of the company and a few details so I could tell Susan about it when she came home from work. Later that evening, I started telling her about the news report on bungee jumping, but before I could finish, she interrupted me to say, *"You are NEVER going bungee jumping!"* Well, I remember being quite surprised by her reaction. After all, I had told her all about my skydiving adventure, and how incredible it was to float back down to earth in silence. Susan knew all about my story, but I could tell by her tone of voice and facial expression that this was new and dangerous ground. We had been married for a year and a half, and had never disagreed on activities or major purchases. As a relatively new husband, however, I felt that I was still learning about being married. I was not going to lie to her and go bungee jumping behind her back. I decided that this must be one of those times where the husband has to compromise, and not do something that his wife is adamantly against. There was a small chance that some type of equipment failure could occur, and she was not going to let me take that risk just for fun.

In hindsight, our ability to respect each other's opinion and compromise, when necessary, would be essential as we faced the trials that were coming our way in the future.

CHAPTER 17

A Family In My Neighborhood

When I was eleven years old, I would play football with a friend who lived down the street from me. He was in the same grade, and we attended the same school. Since we both had younger brothers, we would get them to join us in the games. My friend and his younger brother were healthy, well-behaved, and very smart kids who made the Honor Roll.

One day I found out that his mother was going to have another child. After the baby was born, I learned that the baby had Down's syndrome and other health problems. Several days later, my mother told me that the baby had died.

I asked my mother why this had happened, and she said that sometimes when a woman is over forty, that the baby might be born with serious health problems. My friend's mother was forty-two years old. I remember thinking just how frightening it was to know that my friend's little baby brother had died; I had never experienced anything like that before. I also remember thinking how old being forty-two must be, and I decided that I would make sure to have all my children born before I turned forty years old.

CHAPTER 18

Getting Married and Fighting Infertility

After graduating with a BBA in Management and Finance, I went to work for several large corporations. Being in my twenties and single, it was standard practice that I would be chosen for the position requiring relocation, and that made staying in Atlanta very difficult. Moving to a smaller city meant fewer people to meet, and less to do on the weekends.

After my 30th birthday, I moved back to Atlanta, and I met Susan a year and a half later. We dated several times a week, were engaged in ten weeks, and married in nine months.

Several months after our first anniversary, Susan started having problems with her monthly cycle. She had several appointments with her gynecologist, but nothing was found to be seriously wrong until we started trying to have a child. When she did not get pregnant, her gynecologist referred her to an expert reproductive endocrinologist. He was the top doctor in this field in Atlanta, and I had even seen him on the local news station being interviewed. Our appointment was informative—and devastating. Only a few of the required tests and procedures were covered by our insurance. We would have to pay for everything else. The in-vitro procedures cost between $12,000 and $15,000 each, and it was common at that time for a couple to need five or more cycles to become pregnant. As we did not have $75,000 sitting in a savings account, we thanked the doctor for his time and went home. Susan did her best to chart her morning temperatures, and use the ovulation tests, but nothing worked. It was a very sad time for both of us.

Having infertility is like riding a roller coaster from hell together. Every month, there are ups and downs, twists and turns, and no positive results from the pregnancy test kits. Every month is another lost opportunity to have a child. Even worse is the fact that as each month goes by, the chances of having a child are somewhat less than the month before. As the chances for success go slowly downhill, your hope for the future does too. Infertility becomes an attack against your marriage and your outlook on life.

As you struggle to get pregnant, you must deal with the world around you moving forward. Wherever you go, it seems like you are surrounded by babies. There are babies everywhere! At church, at the grocery store, at the mall, at the park, and on television, there are babies around every corner and in every store—and you can't stop yourself from staring at each and every one of them. And then come the Mother's Day commercials on television, as you sit next to your wife on the sofa, and wonder what she is thinking. But worst of all are the holidays, when you get together with the people you love, and stare at all of the family children in one place. Every year, you see how some children have grown, some have recently been born, and some are almost ready to be born—and you are another year older, and still without children.

On one cold Thanksgiving afternoon at my cousins Victor and Cathey's house, one of the family children, Savannah, sat down next to Susan. After a few minutes of observing all of the people there, this beautiful four-year-old girl looked up at Susan and said, *"Where are Your babies?"* It was a fair question; after all, we were the only married couple there without children. Susan did not know that I had overheard Savannah's question. How would she answer? Or would she get up and run out of the room?

At that moment, my cousin Larry grabbed me and shook my hand, and I did not hear my wife's answer. When I turned around, I was relieved to see that Susan was still talking cheerfully with Savannah. I never told her that I had overheard Savannah's question. Some things are better left alone.

CHAPTER 19

Message From an Angel

Ten years had passed since Susan and I were married, and we had planned an anniversary trip to Williamsburg, Virginia. My father was from Roanoke, and my family drove up from Georgia every year to spend the Christmas holidays with my father's sister, my Aunt Martha, and her family in Salem, Virginia. My parents had taken my brother and me to Williamsburg several times, and I wanted Susan to see it.

Susan had turned forty-one a month earlier, and I had given up on having children. Very few women with fertility problems are able to get pregnant after age forty. However, Susan was still talking about having a child, and had recently had a dream that she was going to have a boy with wavy blond hair. I had patiently listened to her story about this dream, but I did not believe that it would ever come true.

It was a long drive to Williamsburg; we arrived at 11 p.m. Susan went straight to bed, and I got in the shower to relax, since I had driven most of the way. As I stood there, a wave of grief hit me by surprise. I thought to myself, "It's my tenth anniversary, and I still don't have any children—and I never will." The combination of Susan turning forty-one and our tenth anniversary was overwhelming, and I began to cry, and I began to pray, and I asked Jesus over and over, "Oh Lord, where are my children?" The hot water in a hotel never runs out. I stood there for over an hour and was exhausted. Finally, I turned the water off, just stood there for a few moments, and thought to myself, "I'm so sad and tired, and I just want to go to sleep." Suddenly, a warm feeling surrounded me, as if I had just been wrapped in a warm blanket. All the sadness melted away, which was a complete surprise, and totally unexpected. I did not physically see or hear anything, but I felt a Christian presence, and I was given the knowledge of three things:

- My prayers had been heard.

- We were going to have a child—after all these years.

- I was going to be given a poem as an acknowledgement that I still wanted a child, and as a sign that this was really going to happen to me.

I thought that this was very strange, and I thought to myself, "I haven't written a poem since I was a senior in high school, and

I absolutely did not enjoy writing them because of all the tortuous poetry rules. And why would I be writing a poem after midnight when I'm on vacation?" Then the poem started coming into my mind. I started to panic, since I was still standing in the shower, so I quickly dried off, put on some clothes, and looked for a pen and paper to write it down. There was no paper, so I wrote the poem down on the hotel information sheet that listed the room prices. Here is the poem:

OTHER PICTURES

On the bedroom wall I see
Baby pictures watching me.
Three sweet portraits in a row
Each with its hand-crafted glow.
I'd give anything to see
Other pictures—not just me.
For these pictures are my own
Taken in a time long gone
Long before our fate was known.
Even though the seed is sown
We will not have children, for
My wife cannot have children.
I'd give anything to see
Other pictures—not just me.

I wrote the poem down in five minutes. There is no way that I could have ever created a poem like this on my own in just five minutes. I was never any good at writing poetry.

The "Three sweet portraits in a row" line refers to three photographs of me that were taken when I was two years old. These pictures were placed side by side in a single rectangular frame, and had been hanging on the wall for many years. There is no reason why I would ever write a poem about my old baby pictures, especially after midnight when I was tired. This poem was given to me as a sign that we were going to have a child. I did not tell Susan about the poem the next day. I put it away, and decided the time to show her the poem would come later.

CHAPTER 20

It's Positive!
It's Positive!

A few months after our trip to Williamsburg, we were at home, and it was raining. We could not go outside for our bike ride, so I set up the Blackburn bicycle trainer for Susan's bicycle, which allowed her bike to be ridden indoors. She was wearing her Polar heart monitor in order to keep her heart rate in the correct range for an effective workout.

Shortly after Susan started pedaling, the heart monitor began beeping rapidly, which meant that her heart was now beating way too fast. This was very strange, as she had just started her work-out. It scared both of us because we thought that she was having a heart attack. I told her to stop, get off the bike, and suggested that she should ride the next night instead. We both thought that she was just too tired.

The next night, I set up the bicycle trainer for Susan, and the same thing happened again! The heart monitor started beeping rapidly, and indicating that her heart was beating way too fast. We were really stressed out now, because we thought that Susan must have a serious heart condition. I told her that she would have to call her doctor in the morning for an exam. She agreed, and went to take a shower to calm down.

The next day was a busy Friday, and because she was feeling fine, Susan did not make a doctor's appointment. Instead, while on the way home, she stopped at a drugstore and bought a pregnancy test kit. She had read that a fast heart rate was a sign of being pregnant. That night, she made an excuse for not seeing the doctor, and promised that she would go on Monday. The next morning, she finally found enough courage to try a pregnancy test. Susan ran into the living room and yelled, *"It's positive! It's positive!"* I looked up and said, "What are you talking about, and what is that thing in your hand?" She said, "I'm pregnant!" I said, "No, you're not. Go do another one of those tests." The other tests gave the same positive results, and her condition was confirmed by a visit to Dr. Richard C. Zane. We waited a few more weeks to make sure that everything was OK, and then we had a wonderful time calling everyone with the great news. Finally, we were going to have a child! Thanks be to God!

CHAPTER 21

Pregnancy, Delivery, and Choosing a Name

Susan's mother, Jean, had six children, and she did not have a lot of morning sickness during her pregnancies. Susan did not have much morning sickness either, and she was very thankful about that.

Because Susan was forty-one years old, her pregnancy was classified as high-risk. She went through a series of prenatal visits with Dr. Zane. He recommended a battery of tests, including an amniocentesis, which required using a *HUGE NEEDLE* to remove a sample of her amniotic fluid. Susan was very brave, and held perfectly still for Dr. Zane during this procedure. All of the exams and tests were normal, so Dr. Zane told us not to worry.

However, I had two complications during her pregnancy. The first one occurred when our baby really started to kick.

Susan was resting on the bed and showed me where to put my

hand to feel our baby's kick. When I put my hand on her, the baby gave almost the hardest kick of the entire pregnancy. I jumped back at least three feet, and Susan was laughing so hard that I thought she was going to have our baby right then. I leaned over the bed and said in a loud voice, "You're not born yet, and you're already asking to be put on restriction!" Fatherhood was not starting out very smoothly for me.

The second complication occurred when we went to our first evening childbirth class at Dr. Zane's office. We sat down in a large room with about twenty other couples. I looked around the room at all of them, and whispered in Susan's ear, "We look old enough to be the parents of half the people in this class." It was an accurate observation; however, the stern look from my wife let me know that my remark was neither appropriate nor appreciated! I spent the rest of the evening being quiet, helpful, and attentive.

Because everything was going so well, Susan was able to work until two days before our baby was born. Of course, he decided to start things up at 1 a.m. We got in the car, and I was driving at least 60 mph in a 45-mph zone when I flew by a barely hidden police car. Thankfully, I had remembered to turn on the car's emergency flashers for the trip to Northside Hospital. The officer let us pass without incident. Susan was in a lot of pain until she received an epidural block, and then she was able to give birth a little after 1 p.m. I cut the umbilical cord, and then I took some pictures of our new baby boy.

We named him after my good friends from college, John and Mike. I had done some research on boy baby names, and used an Old English form of John: Evan. And so, his name was Evan Michael Messick.

CHAPTER 22

Evan's First Thanksgiving

After a few days, we brought Evan home from the hospital to our apartment. He was happy and well-behaved, but he quickly made a new rule for us to follow: after he was put to bed in his room for the night, absolute quiet was required. Any conversation or other noise louder than a whisper was instantly met with a yell of disapproval. This behavior lasted for about two months, until Evan became more adjusted to his surroundings.

As the days went by, I learned how to take care of Evan, and he learned that I was his Dad. We developed a bond that was truly amazing to me. Susan stayed home for eight weeks, and then I was on my own with Evan. I looked at several of the best accredited daycare facilities close to our neighborhood, but decided that I would stay home with him.

Susan and I had a long conversation about the daycare facilities that I had seen. Those observations, combined with some books that we had read regarding child development, led us to decide that I would stay home with Evan until he was four years old and then I would go back to work full time. I was taking a business class and working part time when Susan became pregnant, and she had just received a big promotion at work, so this seemed to be the right path for us.

About four months after Evan came home from the hospital, it was time to go to Victor and Cathey's house for our family gathering at Thanksgiving. Their house had a large living room, dining room, and family room, so all of our Atlanta relatives would have a place to sit down together.

This was Evan's first Thanksgiving, and everyone was looking forward to seeing him. Susan and I were a little concerned about how Evan would react around two dozen people, but our happy little boy enjoyed all the attention. After awhile, we put Evan on a sofa with Savannah and her younger sister Julie, who was three years old. Both girls were quite taken with Evan, and took turns holding him until Julie said that she didn't want to share Evan with Savannah anymore. When she was asked how she felt about Evan, Julie said, "I want to keep him. He can live in my room." Everyone in the living room laughed at this, and I went into the family room to tell my cousin Walter what Julie had said about Evan. Walter pretended to be upset with Julie's idea, and said, "Oh No. There will be *No Boys* in her room as long as I'm here."

As you remember, Susan described a dream in Chapter 2 about

having a little boy with wavy blond hair. I did not believe that her dream would come true because of her fertility problems, as well as the fact that Susan had almost black hair and I had wavy, dark brown hair. How would we ever have a little boy with wavy blond hair? When Evan was born, he had deep blue eyes and some light brown hair. Four months later, Evan had hazel eyes and lots of wavy blond hair—exactly like Susan's dream.

CHAPTER 23

Evan Helps Us Buy a House

The day after Evan's first Thanksgiving turned out to be a day to remember—for a very different reason. I left our apartment about 5 p.m. and drove up the street to Toys R Us. Five minutes later, Susan thought she smelled smoke and went outside to investigate. She knocked on a neighbor's door, the woman came outside, and they both agreed that they smelled smoke. They walked around for a few minutes, but they could not see any smoke. Even so, the smell was getting stronger. The neighbor went back into her apartment and called 911, and Susan went back inside, called 911 and the apartment manager. Five minutes later, a screened porch on the first floor below our apartment burst into flames, and the fire was quickly spreading straight up the back side of the building. The fire trucks arrived, and a fireman pounded on our door.

He told Susan to "Get out now!" Susan put Evan into his hand-held baby carrier and left the apartment. Smoke had just filled the walkways and the stairs, which made it difficult for Susan to see and breathe while she was carrying Evan down the stairs. The firemen quickly put out the fire, and Susan called my cell phone to tell me what had just happened. I rushed back to our burned building, and then went to another building where Susan and Evan were waiting for me.

After the firemen left, we inspected our apartment and found that it smelled very strongly of smoke. We decided to spend the night in a hotel so that Evan would not be exposed to the strong smell. We opened all the windows and left for the night. We returned the next afternoon and found that the smell was almost gone. Our apartment had escaped the fire, and had no lasting smoke or water damage because it was located on the front side of our building; the back side of the building was the burned side. If Susan had not smelled the smoke when she did, then the entire back side of the building would have been on fire before the fire trucks arrived, and we could have been forced to move out. I told Susan that I was very proud of the way that she had handled the situation.

Unfortunately, this was not the first time that we had experienced a serious problem with our apartment. Three years earlier, on Christmas Eve night, we left our apartment to attend the 11 p.m. service at Peachtree Presbyterian Church. Susan was Catholic, and we were married at Holy Family Catholic Church in Marietta, Georgia. Susan and I would go to her church on one Sunday, and then go to my church, Peachtree Presbyterian, on the next Sunday. But on Christmas Eve, we always went to the candlelight service at Peachtree Presbyterian for the beautiful music program, and to listen to Dr. Frank Harrington give his Christmas Eve sermon.

We returned home just after 1 a.m. and parked in front of our building. As I was about to turn off the car's headlights, I noticed that water was streaming down the sidewalk. I said to Susan, "The maintenance men left the sprinkler system on, and it's freezing outside, so be careful not to slip on some ice." We had lived there for five months, but somehow at that moment, I had forgotten that there was no sprinkler system. As we walked to the front of our building, we saw a river of water splashing down the stairs. Susan looked at me, and then took off running up the stairs. She turned around and yelled, "The water is coming out from under our front door!"

I ran up the stairs, unlocked the door, and opened it. Water poured out and soaked my shoes. I went inside and saw that the lower heating element of the water heater had blown out, and thousands of gallons of water had been pouring into our apartment for hours. I shut off the power to the water heater, and then turned off the water valve on the supply pipe. We stood in our living room, and I got Susan to stop crying by reminding her that we had renter's insurance, so the damage would be covered. On one end of our apartment, the presents under the Christmas tree were soaking wet, and on the other end, all of our shoes in the closet were also ruined. Everything in the apartment that had contact with the floor was just ruined: all the furniture, and my precious stereo speakers! At 9:30 a.m. I called my good friend from college, Rick, who was my State Farm Agent, and told him what had happened. The damage was covered, but it took several months to get everything back to normal.

First the flood, and then the fire. We had been through enough, and it was time to look for a house, especially since we now had our little boy. I did not want to drag Evan along on a lot of trips with a real estate agent to look at the houses. Instead, I would find our house by looking on the internet. Susan and I wanted a typical 3-bedroom, 2-bathroom house, but we also wanted a great room with a small corner fireplace. Finding a house with that floor plan was very difficult, and I spent several hours every day looking for our house. Almost seven months later, on Father's Day, I found an affordable house in a great neighborhood with the right floor plan. It was Sunday afternoon, so we decided to drive over to the house and see if we could have a tour. We knocked on the front door and a very old man opened the door. He did not seem that happy to see us, since we did not have an appointment. Then his wife came to the front door, and she saw Evan and said, "What a beautiful baby! He's the most beautiful baby boy I've ever seen— except for my own children, of course. Please come inside." And so, we were invited to look at the house while she played with Evan in the great room. We loved the house, and told them that we would make an offer the next day.

We closed on the house seven weeks later. It was an attractive little house, painted light gray with a dark gray roof, white trim, and dark royal blue shutters and front door, on a 1/3-acre lot with a backyard large enough for Evan to play comfortably. Evan sat in his stroller, and smiled and laughed as I rolled him through the empty house a few days before our move-in day on August 26, 1999. We had just celebrated Evan's first birthday the month before. Finally, we had our little boy, our house, and new hope for our family's future.

CHAPTER 24

Disaster After Evan's 2nd Birthday

On the day after Evan's 2nd birthday, we were in the kitchen, and I was feeding Evan his lunch. He was sitting in his high chair, and on the countertop next to him were three big stacks of board books which he flipped through as he ate his food. Halfway through lunch, as he was reading a book, instead of finishing the book, he stopped in the middle, closed the book, and looked up at me. I said, "Read your book, Evan." He started reading, stopped in the middle again, closed the book, and looked up at me again. I tried to open the book back to the middle, but he held onto the book and refused to open it. Something clicked in my mind, and I thought to myself, "He isn't finishing this book because he cannot remember his place in the book. He can't remember what he is reading, and so he is starting over again. Something is terribly wrong." I called his pediatrician and spoke with the on-call nurse.

Because it was a Friday afternoon, there were no appointment times left. Since Evan's 2-year check-up was already scheduled for the following Thursday, the nurse said that if anything was wrong, the check-up would discover it. Because Evan was not having any visible physical distress, I decided to wait until his scheduled appointment, hoping that I was wrong, and this problem was just in my imagination.

On the next Thursday, Evan's pediatrician gave him a thorough exam and discovered that his head had grown a little larger than normal. This factor, combined with Evan's losing interest in his toys, and his lack of talking, gave the doctor enough reasons to order a CT scan. As you already know, a cranial arachnoid cyst was found, and Evan had brain surgery to put in a shunt to drain the excess fluid away. After the surgery, Evan was unable to walk or even crawl. He would try to crawl, and then he would look up at me as if to ask, "Why can't I crawl or walk anymore, Daddy?" I kept encouraging him to crawl to me during our playtime. Evan kept trying, and after two weeks he was crawling, and after another month, he was walking again. Six months later, Evan lost his appetite, and three weeks before his 3rd birthday, he was diagnosed with A.L.L., acute lymphoblastic leukemia.

Susan has already discussed Evan's trials with leukemia, and so I don't need to repeat that part of Evan's story. Instead, I have some other stories to tell you.

CHAPTER 25

A River of Gasoline

At the beginning of Evan's chemotherapy treatment, Susan and I would have to make four or five trips from our house to the hospital in order to bring Evan's books, videos, clothes for Evan and me, food, etc. because we had two small four-door sedans. One of us would have to stay with Evan, while the other person would have to bring everything else. This quickly became very annoying, and since our smaller car was quite old, we decided to get a larger vehicle. With years of trips to the hospital ahead of us, we started to wonder if we should buy a minivan.

My good friend from college, John, and his wife, Jonella, had a minivan, and they generously offered to let us drive it for several weeks to see if we liked it. Jonella and her younger daughter, Erin, brought the minivan over to our house.

The minivan seemed fine, but on my first trip with Evan to the hospital, the engine shut off. I pulled over to the side of the road on a very busy Interstate 400 highway during rush hour, and wondered what I should do. Evan had a spinal tap procedure scheduled in 40 minutes, so I decided to call 911. After explaining that my son had leukemia, and that he had a critical medical treatment that he could not miss, a Fulton County Officer was there in 15 minutes. He took us down the interstate to the hospital and dropped us at the front door. (Thanks again for the fast help.) I called John and told him what had happened. He called the dealership, had the minivan towed in for repairs, and then brought it back to our house.

During the next week, Evan had another appointment for chemotherapy, and this time the minivan made the trip with no problems. Evan received several different chemotherapy infusions that day, so we didn't leave the clinic until 5:30 p.m. Evan sat quietly in his stroller as I rolled him through the large parking deck to the minivan. I put Evan into his car seat, got into the minivan, and turned the key—and it wouldn't start.

Having done my own car repairs since I was a teenager, I knew quite a lot about cars. I have replaced ignition systems, alternators, carburetors, fuel pumps, water pumps, etc. and I knew about the different kinds of fuel injection systems. Fuel injection systems usually work perfectly, or not at all. If this minivan wouldn't start right away, it probably wasn't going to start. I knew that—but we were tired, hungry, and wanted to go home, so I kept trying to start the vehicle.

After about ten minutes of trying to start the minivan, an Indian man who was walking by came over to my driver's window and had a terrified look on his face. I put my window down a bit and he said, "There is *a River of Gasoline* coming out from under your car." He turned around and quickly walked away. I jumped out of the minivan, looked underneath it, and ran around to the other side. I took Evan out of his car seat, held him tightly, and took off running until I was at least 100 feet away. There was so much gasoline that it had flowed past the minivan on the floor of the parking deck and made a puddle of gasoline even bigger than the minivan.

I called the main number of the hospital and asked for Hospital Security. I told them what had happened, and that they needed to immediately barricade that section of the parking deck before a car or someone with a cigarette walked by and caused the minivan to catch on fire. Gasoline fumes are heavier than air, can travel across the ground for hundreds of feet, and can ignite with just a spark. Hospital Security officers quickly put up some barricades and began directing traffic. They also had some maintenance workers bring a pickup truck half full of treated sawdust to put on the puddle of gasoline to absorb it. I called Susan, told her to come get us, and called John to tell him what had happened. Time to call the tow truck again.

When the minivan was towed in for service the previous week, the in-line fuel filter had been replaced. It had not been tightened properly, and when I tried to start the minivan, the connection between the filter and the fuel line was spraying gasoline underneath the minivan. If the gasoline had caught on fire before I got Evan out, there is no doubt that we would have been burned alive. I really don't know why it didn't catch on fire, but I certainly said my prayers that night, and thanked God that Evan and I were alive and not burned up.

Susan and I decided that we should buy a minivan, so I looked on the Insurance Institute for Highway Safety website to see the crash test results for minivans, and I looked at my Consumer Reports magazines to see the Frequency of Repair results to find the most reliable vehicle. We bought a different brand of minivan; it was safe and reliable for many years, and was a tremendous help in making trips to the hospital.

CHAPTER 26

Almost Crushed in the Driveway

My deadly close call with John and Jonella's minivan was not the only time that I was saved from disaster. In April of 1978, I was home from college for a weekend visit. On that Sunday afternoon, my grandmother called me and asked that I drive over to her house to put some heavy boxes into her car. She lived in a neighborhood that was only eight minutes away, so this was an easy task to complete.

I drove to her house and parked my car about fifteen feet behind her car in the driveway. I loaded the boxes into her car and then helped her down the front steps of her house. She got into her car and started the engine so the air conditioning would be cooling. I said, "Wait until I pull out of the driveway and then follow me home." She was having supper with us that night, and then I was driving back to the University.

As I turned to walk back to my car, I noticed a big, brown moth was smashed on my car's front license plate. I thought to myself, "That looks really bad. I'm going to pop that dead bug off of my license plate before I drive home." As I took the first step towards my car, a voice inside my head said to me, "You don't need to do that right now." The voice had no emotion, but was making a statement of fact, and somehow, I knew that I should listen and do what I was told to do. Instead of walking to the front of my car, I found myself standing next to the driver's side front wheel, and looking down at my feet. Then I remembered that I was supposed to pop that dead bug off of my car's front license plate. As I turned around, my grandmother backed her car into my car!

I watched in horror as my car's front bumper was being driven back on its supports, and her car's big back bumper was about to hit my car's hood and curl it like a potato chip! She hit the brakes, and then pulled forward about seven feet. I walked back to her window and said, "You were supposed to wait until I pulled out of the driveway, remember?!" We were both shaken up, but my car's front bumper also had a black rubber strip, and both cars had escaped any damage.

As I drove home, it slowly dawned on me that if I had been between the cars when she backed up, that I would have been smashed as flat as that big, brown moth. I never told anyone about what had almost happened. About six months later, my grandmother was in a bad car wreck that was her fault. Her car was totaled, and she never drove again.

CHAPTER 27

Evan Gets a Laptop

After Evan became a year and a half old, he was allowed to start watching television, and I also bought several videogames for my desktop computer that featured Barney and Thomas the Tank Engine. I had an NEC 21-inch CRT monitor on my home office desk, and Evan would sit in my lap, watch the videogames, and pat on the monitor's screen. The monitor was very heavy because of the thick glass screen, so I didn't worry that Evan could hurt himself or the monitor.

During Evan's second year of school, he was introduced to a new kind of monitor: a CRT touchscreen monitor. For the first time, Evan discovered that he could interact with a computer! This was a huge turning point in his education, and he was introduced to the Edmark Reading Program: Level 1. This software was used at school to teach students that had autism, developmental disabilities, or learning disabilities. Evan really enjoyed learning and using this reading program at school, so it was time to find a way for him to use the program at home and in his hospital room.

We had never purchased a laptop before, so I did some online research and decided to buy a Dell Inspiron with a 15-inch screen using Windows XP. Because the laptop did not have a touchscreen, I bought a Keytec Magic Touch add-on touchscreen that attached with Velcro straps and plugged into the USB port. Now Evan had a functional laptop that he could operate, and it was always on unless he was asleep.

Evan took great pride in showing us that he could operate his laptop, and that he had learned the 150 words taught by the Edmark Reading Program: Level 1. After talking with his teachers, we later purchased the Edmark Reading Program: Level 2 software, and that added 200 more words for Evan to learn. He could not say the words, but he understood them. The laptop also allowed Evan to have some entertainment by playing online games from Starfall and watching some of his favorite PBS Kids shows like Curious George and Super Why.

Without a touchscreen computer for Evan to use, we would never have had a window into what Evan was able to learn and understand. We were also able to get a Dynavox assistive communication tablet which was programmed by Evan's speech teacher, and this provided another set of tools for Evan to let us know what he wanted. I will always be so thankful for those devices that let us communicate with Evan.

CHAPTER 28

Don't Delay My Walk

Whenever Evan and I were in the hospital, there were a few things that he looked forward to: seeing the nurses whom he loved, seeing his therapists Kerri, Liz, and Terry, and going on walks inside and outside of the hospital. We walked on every floor, looked at books in the library, and went outside behind the hospital to the koi pond where we would always count the colorful fish. Downstairs in the lobby, there was a huge interactive video display built into the wall, and Evan would press the button over and over to change the video so that he could listen to the next story.

Most of the time during these walks, Evan would be receiving fluids or medicine through IV lines, and I would have Evan's hand in my right hand and the hospital pole in my left hand. We rolled along, and went almost everywhere.

Occasionally, the chemotherapy protocol would allow Evan to be disconnected from the infusion pump for 2 hours. This was always a special time, because now Evan could go on his walk without being attached to the hospital pole.

On one afternoon, the nurse came in and disconnected Evan from the pump. I cleaned him up, put fresh clothes on him, put on his shoes and coat, and we were ready for our walk. At the moment we started to leave, a doctor came into our room, and she wanted to give Evan an exam.

Evan looked up at me, and he had a big frown on his face. He crossed his arms over his chest, and looked up at her with that big frown still on his face. She tried to uncross his arms so that she could open his coat and use her stethoscope, but he would not move his arms even an inch.

I looked at her and said, "We were just leaving for our walk, and Evan has just classified you as a delay." She looked at me, straightened herself, and said in a somewhat loud voice, "I am not a delay!" I started laughing and said, "Look at his face. You've already lost this battle, and it's time for you to make a graceful exit." She looked down at his grim little face and started laughing too. Then she said, "Can you be back in an hour and a half?" I said, "Yes, we can do that." And then she hurried out the door to see her next patient.

On this hospital stay, we were in a room right next to the nurses' station. As we left the room, Evan was holding my hand, and all of a sudden, *he started dancing!* Neither I nor the nurses had ever seen him dance before. He must have learned how to dance at school. All the nurses were laughing, and one of them said, "What's up with Evan?" I said, "He is dancing a Victory Dance, because he refused

to let the doctor give him an exam and delay his afternoon walk."
Evan knew that he had won the argument. He held my hand, and
danced down the hall all the way to the elevator.

After we came back, Evan walked into the nurses' station to
play a game that he had invented: he would go to each nurse who
had her hair in a ponytail, and he would want to see the color of
her elastic hair tie. The nurses knew that when Evan was in the
nurses' station, that the game was on, and ponytails must be pre-
sented for inspection. They were always so kind to take that time
with Evan, and play his game. Evan had always played with Susan's
hair, because when he was a baby, she would tickle his face with
her hair. Playing with the nurses' ponytails was simply another
way for Evan to show that he loved the nurses.

CHAPTER 29

How Much Risk Will You Take?

As you know, Susan had fertility problems for years before our son Evan was born. Having been through these trials with her, I felt compelled to include a chapter in this book which addressed the facts about infertility that I have learned.

This chapter will not apply to everyone reading this book, but for those couples who have lost a child and who plan on having another child sometime in the future, I wanted them to know these facts so that they can make informed decisions.

As you have read, I went skydiving in college, and Susan said that I was *"NEVER going bungee jumping!"* Most couples reduce their risks in life by not going skydiving or hang gliding. Smart couples reduce their risks by making good decisions, like using the Insurance Institute for Highway Safety website to select a vehicle with the best safety features.

But how do you reduce your risks of having fertility problems, or having a child born with birth defects? For both men and women, until you know the facts about infertility, you cannot make informed decisions. This puts any child you hope to have at greater risk— thus the name of this chapter.

For both men and women, age is the most important cause of declining fertility and increased chromosomal defects that can result in miscarriage, autism, and birth defects. Most experts agree that women have about 60% of the fertility problems, and men have about 40% of the fertility problems.

Infertility is brutal and unforgiving. A woman's fertility peaks in her mid-twenties and starts to decline about age 27. Her fertility declines more quickly in her early thirties, and by age 35 about one-third of all women cannot get pregnant without assisted reproductive technology such as ovulation induction combined with intrauterine insemination, or the next step of in-vitro fertilization. After age 35 fertility falls very quickly, and by age 40 about two-thirds of all women cannot get pregnant without using in-vitro fertilization. After age 40, a woman's ability to get pregnant using her own eggs is very low because her eggs are no longer viable: at age 40 half of her eggs have chromosomal defects, and at age 42 about 90% of her eggs have chromosomal defects. The stories in the news about women in their forties using in-vitro fertilization to have children never mention that these children were conceived using fresh donor eggs from a 21-year-old woman; this promotes the idea that age is not important.

There is an ongoing discussion about women deciding to freeze their eggs before they turn 35 years old. This procedure appears to solve the problem of keeping a woman's eggs from getting older until she is ready to have children. However, it is very expensive, and there is no guarantee that the eggs will be viable after they have thawed out. Some eggs tolerate the procedure very well, while other eggs do not produce embryos that develop normally; this puts those women back into the group whose best choice is fresh donor eggs.

Men have their own set of concerns about their fertility, and men have fertility problems almost as often as women. While a woman's age is the most important factor for a couple trying to have a child, the man's age is also important. Even though a man produces new sperm every day, as a man gets older, the quality of the sperm slowly declines. Beginning in his forties, it takes more time for the man to get the woman pregnant—in the bedroom, or by using in-vitro fertilization. A man's age is his main cause of chromosomal abnormalities that can also result in miscarriage, autism, and birth defects.

As you remember, the story in Chapter 17 was about my friend who lost his baby brother. His mother had given birth to healthy children when she was younger, and then at age 42 she had a child with Down's syndrome who died. Evan was born when Susan was also 42 years old, and he had multiple health problems. One of Evan's therapists has a brother whose wife was in her late twenties when she had two healthy daughters, and then at age 40 she had a son who was born with tetralogy of Fallot. This is the most common heart defect in children, and includes 4 serious heart abnormalities which severely reduce the amount of blood that the heart can pump, and also the level of oxygen in the blood. Susan's younger sister, Laura, has a husband named Gordon, and he was born when his mother was 38 years old. Two years later, Gordon's sister was born. She was diagnosed with leukemia when she was 4 years old, and died when she was 6 years old.

It is tragic that the lives of these four children were cut short by the chance of something going wrong because each child's mother was in her early forties when these children were born. There are some other stories that I could share with you, but these stories contain enough grief to make the point. As we have learned, infertility has its own schedule, and having children earlier can help to avoid the serious health problems that sometimes occur because of the mother's or the father's age at the time of their child's conception.

From the time that Evan was diagnosed with leukemia, I have since told hundreds of people about the information contained in this chapter. Some of the people who were single decided to have a more serious attitude about dating. After a few years, they met the right person, got married, and had their first child. Some of the people were already married, and after hearing these stories, decided to have their children. I claim partial responsibility for all those children being born. Do you know someone who needs the facts about infertility? Perhaps you could share these stories, and make a difference.

CHAPTER 30

The Sound of Clocks

After Evan died, every morning when I woke up, the only sound in our house was the sound of clocks ticking. The quiet house always reminded me that Evan had gone away.

I used to wonder why Evan was not born in good health because Susan and I had, of course, said our prayers and asked for a healthy child. We did not imagine that we would all have to endure these ordeals. Now that Evan—and Susan—have died and gone to Heaven, the reasons why these things happened are still beyond my understanding.

In John Chapter 3, Jesus is talking with a Pharisee named Nicodemus. From John 3:3, Jesus said, *"Truly, truly, I say to you, unless one is born again, he cannot see the kingdom of God."* Then from John 3:9-12, 16, Nicodemus said to Jesus, *"How can these things be?"* And Jesus answered his question.

"Are you the teacher of Israel, and yet you do not understand these things? Truly, truly, I say to you, we speak of what we know,

and bear witness to what we have seen, but you do not receive our testimony. If I have told you earthly things and you do not believe, how can you believe if I tell you Heavenly things? For God so loved the world, that he gave his only Son, that whoever believes in him should not perish but have eternal life."

Like Nicodemus, there are so many things that I do not understand: the signs that Susan was given, her dream about having a little boy with wavy blond hair, that she was saved from a propane gas leak in her uncle's cabin, that she was saved from a fatal car wreck on Cobb Parkway in Atlanta, that she was given the 10 years with Evan that she asked for, the signs that I was given, the poem that I was given, that Evan and I were saved from being burned to death in John and Jonella's minivan, and that I was saved from being crushed between the cars in my grandmother's driveway.

Once again from Revelation 21:4, *He will wipe away every tear from their eyes, and death shall be no more, neither shall there be mourning, nor crying, nor pain anymore, for the former things have passed away.*

Now I look forward to the day when I will see Susan and Evan again, and we will go for a walk together, hand in hand as we always did before, and Evan and I will have our first big conversation. Then Susan and I will let him go and watch him run, and not worry anymore about him falling down.

I love you, Susan and Evan.

CHAPTER 31

Our Christian Witness to You

It is my sincere hope that the testimony that Susan and I have given to you through the stories written down in this book will strengthen your Christian faith, and give you a large measure of comfort in the days ahead.

I wrote down almost all of my stories about Evan during the six months after losing him in 2009. These stories have been on my computers, along with notes on index cards, stacks of medical records, and other papers packed away in a large box labeled "Evan's Book."

After discovering that she had Stage 4 breast cancer, Susan took a different approach, and used a small, handheld digital voice recorder to document her stories. After they were dictated, she typed all of her stories into her laptop.

Over the years, Susan's sisters, Mary Ann and Laura, kept politely asking me when this book would be completed. They knew

I had promised Susan that I would get it done, and I knew that they would deliver *punishment* if I didn't get it done. I feel a great sense of relief and satisfaction that it's finished, and I hope this book is a blessing to everyone who reads it.

Since I am a first-time author, I would really appreciate it if you would leave a review of this book on the bookstore's website or the online website where you purchased the book. Susan and I wrote this book to help parents like us who have lost their child, and I want to share our book with every parent who needs it.

Raymond Messick

Acknowledgments

There are literally hundreds of people who helped to take care of Evan, whether he was in the hospital or at school. It is not possible to list all those who deserve thanks, so I have decided to list the doctors and nurse practitioners who were most involved in Evan's care while he was in the Aflac Cancer Center at Children's Healthcare of Atlanta at Scottish Rite. After listing those names, I will list the categories of the other people who provided health care or education for Evan. Sincere thanks to all of you who helped my family.

From Children's Healthcare of Atlanta at Scottish Rite:

- Bradley A. George, M.D.

- Louis B. Rapkin, M.D.

- John Bergsagel, M.D.

- Jeanne Boudreaux, M.D.

- Robert M. Campbell, M.D.

- P. Charlton Davis, M.D.

- Beatrice A. Files, M.D.

- Glen Lew, M.D.

- Claire Mazewski, M.D.

- Patrick S. Spafford, M.D.

From Children's Healthcare of Atlanta at Scottish Rite:

- Colleen Austin, C.P.N.P.

- Pamela Brill, C.P.N.P.

- Melissa Martin, C.P.N.P.

From Pediatric Neurosurgery Associates:

- Andrew Reisner, M.D.

- Roger Hudgins, M.D.

From Children's Center for Digestive Health Care:

- Larry M. Saripkin, M.D.

- Jeffrey A. Blumenthal, M.D.

- Jay A. Hochman, M.D.

- Edith S. Pilzer, M.D.

From Emory University School of Medicine:

- Natia Esiashvili, M.D.

From Roswell Pediatric Center:

- Judith R. Tolkan, M.D.

Organizations that fight cancer:

- CURE Childhood Cancer

- The Leukemia & Lymphoma Society

People who provided health care or education for Evan:

- Surgeons

- Family Nurse Practitioners

- Physician Assistants

- Nurses of all Specialties—on duty at all hours every day.

- Nurse Technicians

- Child Life Specialists

- Clinical Case Managers

- Clinical Laboratory Technologists

- Clinical Operations Managers

- Clinical Social Workers

- Clinical Utilization Managers

- Registered Dietitians

- Neuropsychologists

- Occupational Therapists

- Physical Therapists

- Speech-Language Pathologists

- Paramedics

- Pathologists

- Patient Services Managers

- Program Coordinators

- Radiologic Technologists

- School Teachers

- School Teachers' Paraprofessionals

Good Friends and Neighbors

In the last months of his second year of chemotherapy, Evan was having a very difficult time. Our schedules were hectic, and our close neighbors, Lynda and Allan Hoheisel, organized a neighborhood group to cook meals for us. Ten families started bringing us supper twice a week! They didn't just bring us a single dish; this quickly turned into a friendly competition of who was going to bring us the best supper: these meals had a main dish, two vegetables, salad, bread, and dessert. The neighborhood group generously provided meals for four weeks, and then asked if we needed them to continue. Susan and I thanked them for their help, but declined to ask for more meals because Evan was almost over this demanding part of his chemotherapy. We were very fortunate to have such good friends and neighbors helping us at a difficult time.

North Point Mall Merry-Go-Round

Soon after Evan's 4th birthday, I started taking him to the North Point Mall in Alpharetta, Georgia after lunch each day. We went in the early afternoon to ride the merry-go-round because other children would still be in school. Fewer kids meant less exposure to whatever colds they might have that could make Evan very ill while he was having chemotherapy. Evan quickly charmed all the women on the merry-go-round staff with his big smile and gentle hugs. He loved riding the merry-go-round and the women who operated it; they became his special afternoon friends.

After Evan's 5th birthday, he started going to school since his chemotherapy was less severe. After school, we still went to ride the merry-go-round, and then went to Webb Bridge Park to play on the swings, forts, and slides each day.

Soon after Evan's 7th birthday, the leukemia came back, so Evan couldn't go to the mall and ride the merry-go-round anymore. The women who operated the merry-go-round—Stella, Cindy, Loretta, Pat, Mary, Meghan, Robin, and Susan—went to see Stacy, the Marketing Manager for North Point Mall. They told her about Evan, and a plan was made. The mall's Director of Operations, and Head of Maintenance, took an extra, full-size carousel horse and completely painted it, mounted it on a shiny brass pole, bolted the pole to a 3 ft. by 5 ft. painted wooden base, and brought this to our house!

What a wonderful gift for Evan! However, there was a problem: since it was already assembled, it was too big to fit through the front door! They took the horse and pole off of the base, and reassembled it in Evan's playroom (our small dining room). Doesn't everyone have a large carousel horse in their dining room? Now Evan had his own carousel horse, and he would sit on his horse every day and watch television.

I wanted to thank these people at North Point Mall for their incredible kindness, and thank these women who made a wonderful difference in Evan's life with their love and all the special attention they gave to him.

Forsyth County Fire Station 14

At the Christmas after Evan's 4th birthday, he received a big, red Tonka fire truck. Several months later, I took Evan to the Forsyth County Fire Station 14 to see a real fire truck. We met some of the firemen, and every day after that for almost the rest of Evan's life, we would end our day with an evening trip to the fire station. We would park in a special parking place, and a fireman would open the big door in front of the fire truck and turn on the fire truck's flashing lights for two minutes. It was always a great treat at the end of the day. I wanted to thank the firemen at Station 14 for giving Evan those two special minutes every day.

Special Olympics Forsyth County

After Evan started attending school, he also participated in the Special Olympics programs in Forsyth County. After Evan passed away, the Special Olympics Forsyth Coordinator called me to say that the 2009 Forsyth County Spring Games would be dedicated to Evan and another boy named Stephen.

The 2009 Local Spring Games were held on April 17th and official programs that were handed out stated on the front page that these games were dedicated to Evan and Stephen. Inside the program, both families were given a half page for a picture, a caption, and 5 lines for a message about their child. I wanted to thank Special Olympics and Forsyth County for remembering Evan at these games in such a meaningful way.

2009 Daves Creek Elementary Yearbook

I went to the 2009 Local Special Olympics Spring Games and took pictures of Evan's classmates as they participated in the games. I gave the pictures to Evan's teacher, Erin Downey, the following week. I went back to Daves Creek Elementary on the last day of school to see Erin and her paraprofessional, Josephine Plinck. As I was leaving, Erin said that she had a surprise for me. She took me to the school office and handed me a 2009 school yearbook. On page 3, below the pictures of the two assistant principals, was a dedication: "In Memory of our friend Evan Messick." Below those words were four pictures of Evan. I didn't know that there were any pictures of him in the yearbook because Evan had been sick on both school picture days, so I had not ordered a yearbook; of course, I bought this one. I wanted to thank the Daves Creek Administration for honoring Evan in the 2009 yearbook.

America's Most Beautiful Bike Ride

Evan's last teacher, Erin Downey, has a sister named Lisa Downey Blecker. Lisa and her husband, Steve, participated in a 100-mile bike ride around Lake Tahoe on June 7, 2009. They were Team in Training participants, riding to raise funds for The Leukemia & Lymphoma Society, and they both had a picture of Evan attached to the back of their bicycle jerseys during their long ride. Lisa and Steve's fundraising website received donations from 98 people for a total of $5,055 given in Evan's memory. There were over 3,400 participants in this huge event; over half were riding for Team in Training, and they raised a total of $6,800,000 for The Leukemia and Lymphoma Society. I wanted to thank Lisa and Steve for their hard work of getting ready to ride in a 100-mile race, for wearing Evan's picture, and riding in his memory.

The Neighborhood Memorial Tree

After Evan passed away, Lynda and Allan Hoheisel went to our neighborhood Home Owners' Association Board and volunteered to raise money for a Memorial Tree Project that would remember Evan and the eleven other people in our neighborhood who had also passed away. The HOA Board approved the project, and Lynda and Allan raised the money from the neighborhood residents. In late November of 2009, a Japanese maple was planted by the tennis courts near the neighborhood exit. At the base of the tree, a metal plaque with Evan's name and the names of the other eleven residents was installed. A semi-circular wall of brick pavers was installed in front of the tree. The tree was quite small when it was planted, but it has grown to full size and is almost twelve feet tall. The HOA Board thanked Lynda and Allan in the newsletter sent to the neighborhood residents. I wanted to thank Lynda and Allan for their time and dedication to the Memorial Tree Project, and also thank those residents who made this project possible through their financial donations.

Videos for Children in the Hospital

In early 2010, Evan's teacher, Erin Downey, organized a DVD and VHS tape drive in Evan's memory. Each room in the Aflac Cancer Center at Children's Healthcare of Atlanta at Scottish Rite had a combination player that could play both DVDs or VHS tapes. Erin was very successful in inspiring the students at Daves Creek Elementary: they donated 184 DVDs and 268 VHS tapes. Erin also contacted some teachers that she knew at Suwanee Elementary School, and their students donated 39 DVDs and 134 VHS tapes.

The total for both schools: 223 DVDs and 402 VHS tapes equals 625 videos! This video project ended on March 31st, and Erin called me to say that it was time to come and pick up all the videos and take them to the hospital. I called Dr. George and told him that I was bringing 625 videos to the hospital in my minivan.

It took several trips; I was thankful that I had a hand truck to roll all those boxes from the parking deck into the hospital. I wanted to thank Erin Downey for her efforts in organizing this project, and thank the students (and parents) for the gifts of all the videos for children in the hospital.

My Cousin Linda

As you remember, the story in Chapter 6 was about Evan's memorial service. My cousin Linda played her guitar, sang two songs, and the second song was, "Silent Night." Susan used to sing that song to Evan every night at bedtime. I wanted to thank Linda for performing those two songs at his memorial service. She played and sang beautifully; everyone enjoyed her music, and Susan's younger sister, Laura, mentions Linda's performance in the last letter of this book.

My Son Evan

While attending Sharon Elementary School, Evan was given a very special award: he was made a Sharon Knight, which acknowledged his remarkable improvements at school.

Letters Read Aloud at Evan's Memorial Service

Mrs. Terry

I had the joy of meeting Evan when he was two years old. I remember my first therapy session with him. I walked into his house and saw a precious little bald-headed, long-legged boy sitting in his high chair, watching Barney while getting his G-tube feeding. From my first interactions with him, I could tell what a loving and gentle spirited child he was. As the weeks and therapy sessions passed, I built a strong bond with Evan. I loved spending time with him, and seeing his excitement when his favorite Barney DVDs were played, and engaging him in play with his toys.

After seeing Evan at his home for a couple of years, my job changed and I began working at Scottish Rite. As a result, I was unable to see Evan anymore. However, I would still often think of him, and I would receive Christmas cards with his picture on them. I still have one hanging at my desk today.

Unfortunately, as time passed, Evan's leukemia returned and he began getting admitted at Scottish Rite hospital. During his admissions, I was able to once again see sweet Evan for therapy. Every time Liz (Occupational Therapist) and I would go pick him up for therapy, he would jump up and get his shoes on. It didn't seem to matter how sick he was, he was always ready to get out of that small room and play.

Even though Evan didn't have any true words, he was certainly able to use his voice and vocalize in an attempt to get his message across. You could tell by his intonation, expression, and gestures if he was happy or mad with you. He would tell lots of stories by using long sentences of connected sounds, vowels, consonants, clear expressions, and gestures.

Evan was a very sweet child, but we can't forget his ornery side. It was so much fun to work with Evan and watch those wheels turning in his head. I would give him a task to do, and he would purposely do it wrong, and then giggle and look at me as if to say, "What are you going to do now?" It was all I could do to keep a straight face!

Evan was very gentle and loved to be affectionate in his own way. He would hold your hand and make sure that he was sitting right up against you when sitting next to you.

I was so blessed to have gotten the opportunity to spend time with Evan. Most of all, I will remember Evan for his gentle spirit and perseverance to fight such a long battle, and he will always have a very special place in my heart.

Mrs. Terry
Speech-Language Pathologist
Children's Healthcare of Atlanta at Scottish Rite

Susan Wiles

My memories of sweet Evan:

- Big beautiful eyes and a gorgeous smile.

- The way his face lit up when his mom or dad walked into the room.

- The large Little Tikes slide in your foyer so we could work on coordination, balance, and climbing the stairs. He loved the slide, and was proud when he climbed up.

- Evan worked hard, liked to learn, didn't give up, and was not easily frustrated.

- He loved to ride his bike slowly, and we worked on pedaling, steering, and endurance.

- Evan LOVED to play chase.

- He loved watching his TV shows.

- Evan was always happy and always smiling.

- Evan went to the park and went to ride the carousel more in his shortened life than most people ever do.

- He was playful and liked to tease during therapy.

- Evan touched the hearts of everyone he met.

- Evan had the most devoted and loving parents on earth.

Susan Wiles

After School Occupational Therapist

Justine Glover

Your beautiful boy is a vivid memory for me. I picture him today TALKING; of course, I would. He can live on now, be your angel, and look after you the way you have both so diligently looked after him. This boy had FUN despite his medical challenges because his parents were totally devoted to him. You were given a divine job, and you did your job well.

My memory of Evan is that he was happy. Despite his limitations, he responded to playful teasing (Oh yes, you can try this, Mr. Evan!) with a smile. Evan was playful. Treatment sessions with Evan were fun because he didn't get mad or frustrated. He would keep trying so that we could keep playing. Evan was also a great looking kid! That gorgeous thick hair and that handsome face would charm anyone.

Ray and Susan created a comfort zone in Evan's worlds of home/school/hospital, and he was able to relax and enjoy life. Isn't that what we ultimately want for our children? To relax and enjoy? Evan did enjoy his life which included big love. I was privileged to work with Evan and his parents.

Love,
Justine Glover
After School Speech-Language Pathologist

Traci Avery

In 2003, a very special boy came into my life, Evan Messick. He was a student of mine at Sharon Elementary School in Cumming, GA. I remember meeting with Evan's dad, Ray Messick, before Evan started school. Ray told me everything that I would need to know about Evan, and informed me that I would be Evan's first teacher. After meeting with Ray, I was determined to make school a very special experience for Evan, but little did I know that it was going to be the complete opposite. Evan made it a very special experience for me! An experience that has left a lasting impression in my heart forever.

I would like to share with you some of the wonderful memories that I have of Evan at school:

- Evan was an exceptionally happy student. His beautiful smile would light up any room he walked into. I can still see that smile!

- Evan was a hardworking child. He would attempt any task or skill that I asked of him. The one that stands out the most was learning to eat with a spoon. This was a difficult task for Evan, but he was finally able to do it.

- Evan had special ways of communicating his wants and needs to me. We were a great pair!

- Evan would cover his ears to let me know that it was too loud in the classroom or cafeteria.

- Evan would clap his hands and rock in his chair to let me know when he was excited and enjoying an activity. He would do this when we would learn through music.

- He would walk up out of nowhere, give me a big hug, and then smile at me just to let me know he cared. He was a very loving child.

- Evan would get his book bag off the rack to let me know that he was ready to go home.

- Evan was a very strong child. He rarely complained even when he had an uncomfortable medical procedure. He would still come to school and give it his all!

- Evan was a very clean child. He did not like anything on his clothes or face (water, food, etc.), and he made sure that I kept the tables clean. I always told him that I needed him at my house to help with the cleaning.

- Evan was a very social child and loved to go on walks around the school. He would hold my hand and lead me to see what everyone else in the school was doing.

- Evan had the cutest giggle. He would get so tickled and could not stop laughing.

- Evan had a tremendous amount of love for his parents. I got to witness the most precious bond a father and son could ever have every morning and afternoon when Ray would bring and pick up Evan. He became so excited because he knew his dad was picking him up. I could tell by Evan's body language that his dad was his hero!

- Evan had the most caring and loving parents, and they were always there for him. I thank Susan and Ray for entrusting me with Evan, and allowing me to have a special relationship with him.

I will always cherish the memories that Evan and I had together, and there will always be a special place in my heart for him. I love you, Evan!

Traci Avery
Special Education Teacher
Sharon Elementary School

Linda Avolio

It has been several years now since I worked with Evan, but I have never forgotten him. Evan had a special smile that endeared me to him the first minute that I laid eyes on him.

Evan had big sparkling eyes that watched carefully as songs were sung, colors and letters were introduced, and life skills were demonstrated. When Evan began to participate in academic tasks, he would hurry and seem almost impatient to complete them as if he wanted to get on with the next thing to learn, as if he already knew but could not let me know. I began to see that Evan was quite bright, and immediately wanted to explore the possibility of reading skills with him.

I will never forget the first day that I showed Evan the computer program called Edmark Reading Program: Level 1. It was a reading program that began with matching skills and proceeded sequentially with letters, words, and sentences. Evan actually made audible sounds of excitement as he was able to work through the first stages of this reading program. He would touch the screen, locate the answer, and then look to me for approval. I treasure that moment with Evan to this day because it was the first time that he had shown me real communication and excitement over a learning experience.

I got tears in my eyes as I realized that the computer could be a vehicle of communication with Evan, and open new doors for him.

I gave him a hug as I turned off the computer. Evan kept touching the screen as if to say, "I am not finished, and I want to tell you more." That was the beginning of a new time for Evan. His favorite time was working on the computer. I will miss you, Evan. Put a good word in for me with the Lord.

The other thought that remains with me concerning Evan is the love that he had for his father. I waited with Evan after school until his father arrived to take him home. Evan would recognize the car from far away and would begin waving his hands, smiling and pointing to the car until the moment that the car stopped in front of us. He could hardly wait for his father to get out of the car. Evan would rush up and grab onto his father. Ray would immediately pick him up and hug him. It was always a touching scene. Evan would get into the car and want to be on his way. If Ray stopped to talk with me for a minute, Evan would let us know that he needed to get going, and that we should talk later.

Evan was a very special child who touched my life and left an indelible mark. I am a gentler and more sensitive person because of Evan. May God bless his soul.

Linda Avolio
Teacher's Assistant
Sharon Elementary School

Anna Judd

My name is Anna Judd. I was Evan's teacher at Sharon Elementary for the 2004-2005 and 2005-2006 school years. Evan was a blessing to all of us who worked with him. He brought so many joys to my teaching and I have many nice memories of my time spent with him. Ray has talked about how Evan lived in three worlds...school, home, and hospital. I think what Evan enjoyed about the school world was that it gave him the opportunity to do things for himself and be more independent. His place to shine...and that he did.

It was my job to present learning in a variety of ways for Evan, and it was easy to see that he could have done without seatwork assignments. His stubborn side would start to show. It was his way of letting me know that the work was boring, not much fun, and he'd rather be doing something else. But he humored me and we always got through it with the promise of what he really wanted to do...use the computer.

The computer was a great incentive for Evan. He became quite a technology savvy fellow, and much of his learning took place with the assistance of the computer. He worked on reading, math, and writing assignments on the computer, but if I would have let him, he would have sat in front of the computer all day and played on the Starfall website!

Another one of Evan's favorite classroom activities was morning group time. He was fascinated with the days of the week, the months of the year, and dates. He would squirm around in his seat in anticipation of me asking the questions, "What day is today?" and "What month is it?" He'd use his communication board to answer my questions and he was right every time! Evan enjoyed the calendar at school so much that Ray and Susan got him one for home too.

Some of my favorite memories weren't those of Evan's academic success, but more so those little things in life, like riding the school bus for instance. It took a long while to convince Ray and Susan that Evan was ready to ride the bus to school. Like any parents, they had their concerns, and I certainly understood, so I remained patient. As they saw Evan gain some independence that school year, they became more comfortable with the idea of him riding the bus, and much to my delight agreed to let him give it a shot.

Evan was already intrigued by big trucks and semis (I knew this by his obsession with books about big rigs), so it only made sense that he'd find a great big yellow bus just as fabulous. He did... Evan loved riding the bus. It was a big day when he got off the bus by himself and headed for the classroom. And after a long day of work, nothing sounded better to Evan in the afternoon than hearing, "It's time for the bus." A big smile would appear because he knew he'd be heading to his favorite place of all real soon...*home.*

Evan also enjoyed running errands for me and visiting all the office ladies. He had them wrapped around his finger. One flash of that big smile and the ladies were sucked in by his cuteness. One particular errand that became part of his daily routine became quite a big milestone for Evan in the way of independence. His job was to deliver the attendance sheet to Mrs. Hazelwood's office each morning.

He first started out with an adult accompanying him on his journey to show him the way and keep him on task. Over the next few days, the adult would go halfway and peek around the corner to make sure he was focused and on his way rather than stopping along the way to check out the library (one of his favorite places).

Finally, the day came when I was able to ask Evan to take the attendance to Mrs. Hazelwood on his own. Of course I made a call to the office like a worried parent to let her know that he was on his way and on his own. As it turned out, the phone call was not necessary. Evan completed his job and returned to the classroom promptly all on his own. You could see how proud he was of himself that day by the extra pep in his step and his big grin.

This was just a small look inside of Evan and his school world. Evan was a very special guy, and my memories of him will be with me always. Those in his school world loved him very much. I hope we taught him as much as he taught us...

Anna Judd
Special Education Teacher
Sharon Elementary School

Karen Riley

My name is Karen Riley, and I had the pleasure of meeting Evan when Sharon Elementary opened in late 2003. Evan was 5 years old, and I believe he was attending school for the first time. He was scared and unsure of school like many 5 year olds. Evan was truly a joy to see every day walking the halls.

I worked as a Paraprofessional in Special Education, and I also worked at Children's Healthcare of Atlanta as a Patient Care Technician. I was not in Evan's class at school, but because of my training at Children's, I was asked to assist Evan's teacher with his daily G-tube feeds. I was happy to help. Ray was very good about sending all the equipment and formula daily.

Evan was gifted in many ways beyond his years, and also was a fast learner. During his G-tube feeds, we would sit and read magazines; not just any kids' magazines, they were Parents Magazines. Evan loved the computer, was eager to learn, and loved going to school.

While working these two jobs, I also got to see the medical side of Evan on his countless visits to the hospital. Ray and Susan had a system using boxes filled with all the items they would need to keep life as normal as possible during their long admissions to Children's. As I mentioned before, Evan was way beyond his years in some of his interests: some of his videos brought from home were about architecture and home improvement.

Despite Evan's differences and illness, I always thought that he would grow up and become very successful in life. Unfortunately, God had another plan for Evan. I know God has a plan for all of us, and Evan is looking down at us right now, whole and well.

I know Ray and Susan are the best parents and are hurting because their beloved Evan isn't with them in body, but he is with them in mind and spirit. He is not hurting any longer, and is living a much better life than we could ever ask for.

I am so lucky to have met this amazing family, and had a very small part in their lives. I love you Evan, Ray, and Susan.

Karen Riley
School Nurse
Sharon Elementary School

Melissa Martin

I talked to Dr. George this morning, and certainly would like to acknowledge how deeply saddened we are, and how much we miss Evan already. He brought a smile to everyone's face just by the mere mention of his name. He always made his presence known immediately upon arriving at AFLAC, and we all looked forward to his hugs.

The absolute delight he would experience by watching his PBS television shows, participating in his therapies, and playing on his computer was contagious to anyone who had the opportunity to care for him. He left an everlasting impression on all of us, and we will always remember him as an official AFLAC mascot.

Our thoughts and sympathies are with you and your family.

Melissa Martin
Nurse Practitioner
AFLAC Cancer Center at Scottish Rite

Pamela Brill

We all had a special place in our hearts for Evan. He visited us every week (at least) for the last few years, and we always knew exactly how Evan was feeling based on how loud and exuberant he was in the exam room. Our office is right next to the exam room, and we used to know when Evan arrived way before we got paged.

We would hear Evan chattering to Ray and to the TV program in his sing-song voice. As soon as we walked into the room, his face lit up and he would give us this giant smile, followed by a hug or a pat on the cheek. If we were wearing ponytails, he would grab the rubber band and loudly announce what color it was, which always gave him a good laugh.

Evan was so patient while we poked and prodded. As long as he could hold our hands and look into our eyes (or at Barney), he was just fine. What amazed us about Evan was how he played his computer games. The speed and dexterity! He was truly in his element in front of a computer screen. He would turn away from it for a few minutes to give you a heart-melting smile.

Even when Evan's body was failing, his personality never dimmed. He was gentle and loving until his last day. All of us here at AFLAC will miss Evan deeply, and were honored to have been given the opportunity to love and care for him.

Pamela Brill
Nurse Practitioner, AFLAC Cancer Center at Scottish Rite

Edie Borges

You know what I remember most about Evan is the way his little handsome face lit up when he saw the nurses with a ponytail. He also enjoyed taking walks with his dad around the hospital. I will miss seeing that.

Ray and Susan, you were great parents. I will keep you in my prayers.

Love,
Edie Borges
Nurse Tech
Children's Healthcare of Atlanta at Scottish Rite

Jaime Cooke

I so enjoyed taking care of Evan for the past several years. Evan was such a happy, loving kid, and I think one of my very sweetest memories of him happened only recently. Ray called me into the room because Evan simply wanted to see me. When I went in to see Evan, he just wanted to hold hands and be loved on.

It was so precious because he picked up his pillow and moved himself over the edge of the bed just to be close to me. I kneeled down by his bed and held his hand and stroked his hair. It was just a simple and sweet request on his part. Those are the kinds of moments for which one goes into a profession like nursing.

I've always been impressed by how well you two took care of Evan. Although Evan couldn't say the actual words, I know that he loved you both tremendously. He lived a short but very happy life in the midst of all sorts of obstacles. He had fun doing all of the things that kids should do—playing in the park, seeing Christmas lights, watching favorite movies.

You both were wonderful parents to Evan, and should have no doubts about that ever. I know you will miss him. Know that he will always be remembered with great fondness by his nurses and never forgotten. Please keep in touch with us.

Jaime Cooke
Registered Nurse
Children's Healthcare of Atlanta at Scottish Rite

Liz Brown

Where do I begin? From the moment I met this bundle of energy, who LOVED books and trying to rope us into his favorite on campus activities, I was smitten.

We loved to go to the koi pond and count the fish, all the while Evan didn't realize that asking him to follow multiple-step directions and sequence activities was therapeutic. Then once the new hospital lobby was built, how great to go and explore, having Evan work on visual motor and visual-perception skills by simply finding the right button to push, the right sequence of colors, or sequence of animals.

I think that is part of the reason we loved seeing Evan. Clearly, we were bummed if he had a fever or was getting more chemotherapy, but he simply was so happy to see us that it was impossible not to be happy to see him. And most recently, he had progressed from barely copying a line to writing my name just by telling him the letters!! I was so proud of him, and that piece of paper still hangs over my desk. (It was on October 17th.)

The days Evan wasn't feeling so great you could just tell, and that broke my heart. I'd walk into his room and he just looked so sad, he looked as though he REALLY wanted to play, but his body just wouldn't cooperate that day. But when he was on the mend, poor dad couldn't put Evan's shoes on fast enough for him. And Evan couldn't try to run out of the room fast enough, knowing full well that he was in for fun. And I think that dad enjoyed the break, too!

I am most saddened to know that I won't get to see him wave at me again, hear him count the floors while riding on the elevator, or hear him try to say hello with his trademark "Ah-ha" greeting. Evan was an incredibly special young man who has touched my heart and my career in a way that few have even come close. I will miss him terribly and think of him often. Please know that he is light that shines for me always.

Much gratitude for the opportunity to know your son.

Liz Brown "Miss Liz"
Occupational Therapist
Children's Healthcare of Atlanta at Scottish Rite

Jessie M. Schares

Here are a few things that come to mind when I think about Evan...

Everyone knew and loved Evan here at school. He was the smiling young boy who was always in a good mood, always wanted to help, and was always eager to learn something new. Evan was very perceptive and talented. He loved school and always wanted to do his best. We loved to watch Evan's face light up whenever he got excited. (This was usually over something like a favorite show like "Super Why" or a new computer trick he just learned.)

As I reflect back on my time with Evan, I know that it was my honor, privilege, and blessing to have been a part of his life. There is only one angel like Evan, and I will always remember him for the special person he was, the wonderful examples he set, and the great memories he left with us...

Jessie M. Schares
Speech-Language Pathologist
Shiloh Point Elementary School

Betsy Dennison

What I will always remember about Evan was the joy in his eyes! I had the good fortune of having Evan in one of my art classes, and without a doubt, it was the bright spot in my day. Even though Evan could not verbalize his thoughts, he was able to communicate his enthusiasm and love of art to the rest of the class.

He inspired me as well as his fellow classmates. This I rarely see these days. The students enjoyed having Evan in class, and when he was absent for a while, they asked about Evan, and made him a large "Get Well" card!!

Evan will be truly missed but never forgotten. His star will always shine as brightly as one of the stars in Vincent van Gogh's "Starry Night."

Betsy Dennison

Art Teacher
Shiloh Point Elementary School

Lucy C. Nutt

Words cannot adequately express what could be said about the angelic Evan Messick. He was a delight to all who knew him. I had the honor and privilege to know him closely for about a year. During that time, he taught me the true meaning of living each day to the fullest.

Although he couldn't speak in words, he knew right where to push the cell that said "Super Why" or "Fetch" (two of his favorite shows) on his augmentative communication device. He definitely communicated his wants and needs in the most appropriate manner possible. The last few times that I saw him, he gave my arm a light touch to let me know he wanted to connect with me. I will never forget those moments as long as I live.

Never have I witnessed such devotion by a father, and I've known many fathers in my lifetime! No matter what kind of day they had, Ray managed to get Evan to my office in the late afternoon to see how Evan's communication device could be customized to further improve its performance.

Ray and Evan exemplified the true meaning of love and mutual respect. Susan unselfishly took on the role of main breadwinner in the family, often getting home at 9:00 at night after a long, exhausting day. This family deserved so much better, but handled the cards they were dealt with grace and dignity. They helped Evan to fight his fight tirelessly until his very last breath.

May we all cherish the all-too-short life of Evan Messick, and may God be with Ray and Susan during the most difficult time of their already challenged lives. Evan was a GIFT from God to all of us.

Lucy C. Nutt

After School Speech-Language Pathologist

Josephine Plinck

When I first met Evan, he was having a difficult time with his transition to us at Daves Creek Elementary. After a few weeks, we got into a great rhythm. I loved watching him on the computer. He was proficient and confident, and would navigate himself around. He loved one on one work with me. He would bang on the table and want more work.

He knew exactly what he wanted, though I had to learn the cues, which he taught me. The time I spent getting him cleaned up: he knew his personal hygiene routine perfectly, and if I did something out of sequence, he would let me know.

When he became weak, he would lay his head down on me. When I asked him if he wanted to go home, he would become agitated and gesture NO. I truly believe he wanted to come to school, not because of me, but because of his love of learning.

We would walk the halls for a change of scenery. He would wave to the passing students and staff when they said "Hi" to him. I know in situations like this, parents would take their kids to Disney World or to the zoo, but school was Evan's Disney World. He loved being here, and I loved teaching him. (Even though I think I learned more from him.)

I am comforted in knowing that Evan died at home in his earthly father's arms, and now he is in the arms of his Heavenly Father.

Evan will be missed. He has left an indelible mark on all who met him. Thank you for allowing me into his life.

Josephine Plinck

Teacher's Assistant

Daves Creek Elementary School

Erin Downey

Evan entered my life and turned my world upside down. I only saw him at school, but he followed me home. I knew by my first meeting with him that he held a permanent spot in my heart.

His dedication to attend school was immeasurable. Some days were obviously harder than others; but through all of Evan's treatments, the good days and bad days, his fight was deeper than we could have understood. He loved coming to school, doing morning songs, completing his work, and being around his classmates. His laughter at school was contagious. Evan's laughter roared when others got into trouble. The kids loved his laugh.

My favorite memory is when we would wait for the bus together. Evan would hold my hand, and rest his head on my shoulder; he was beat, but happy. I knew that he and his parents had accomplished what they had sought out to do... get Evan well enough to attend school.

Another good memory was Evan showing us what he really knew. When he would type on the computer, he would spell words so well, or when he used his communication device, he would be able to communicate with us so well. All of his teachers, and his reading buddy, Tyler, were amazed. Evan was particular with everything we did for him; he would often put us in our place, which would only make us laugh.

Evan walked into my life, and everyone thinks about how much he loved Mrs. Plinck and me. I hope that I meant half as much to him as he meant to me. He is forever in my heart.

Erin Downey
Special Education Teacher
Daves Creek Elementary School

Kerri Applegate

Ray,

I am so sorry to hear about the passing of Evan. Please know that you and your family are in my thoughts and prayers. Unfortunately, I will not be able to make it to the memorial service, as I am expecting my first child any time now. I'm sorry that I will not be present. Please know that I'll be with you guys in spirit. I did, however, want to share a few of my thoughts about Evan, and I appreciate you including me in this celebration of his life.

Evan was an easy patient to see because his dad always called to inform us of his arrival to the hospital, and to request that therapy begin as soon as possible. Evan always got excited about therapy, and had a smile on his face when he came down to the hospital gym.

I loved that Evan always held my hand on his way to and from the gym; he was such a sweetheart. Evan always went to Mrs. Terry's office to see if she was around. Evan loved to bounce on the therapy balls, and race on the scooter boards.

I hope you will find comfort in your precious memories of Evan. We all have another angel watching over us now.

With Love,
Kerri Applegate
Physical Therapist
Children's Healthcare of Atlanta at Scottish Rite

I want to close the book with this letter from Susan's sister,

Dr. Laura Gottfried

Dear Susan and Ray,

Thank you for sending me the compact disc recording of Evan's memorial service. Today was the first day that seemed like a good day to listen to it, since I had the day off; the kids are at school and Gordon is at work, and I didn't want to have a lot of distractions. They can listen to it later.

I was writing to add my voice to all of those on the recording who expressed thanks for having known Evan, and the recognition of the love and enormous support that you gave him day in and day out. We will remember the time we spent with Evan as well, vividly and with fondness. I am sure that no one else will ever take my hands and put them back over the piano keys to play a song again, something very small and yet very touching to me. It is amazing to think of how many times Evan had such interactions with both of you. We all felt your pain as well, and wished so much that we could make things easier for you. Our prayers for you will continue as the years go on, that you both may find comfort and peace until you meet Evan again.

It was a beautiful service. The Scripture readings and songs were so touching; I'm sure they said it all for you, as much as words can say. The stories and impressions Evan left on so many people are heartwarming. During the Silent Night song, our little dog Spice climbed into my lap sleepily, and I could imagine you holding Evan, and me holding my sleepy babies again to the tune of this lullaby. Those years of having a small child are so precious.

You are both a testament to true love, not only for Evan, but also for each other, since your marriage has survived what has destroyed many others. We hope and pray that the blessing of Evan is one that keeps you close always. I'm sure Evan wishes the same, and has first-hand petition strength in Heaven where he is now; where we all hope to be someday. I'm sure being the happy kid that Evan was, he also wants you to be happy and enjoy life, enjoy the memories of being with him, and look forward to all the times ahead when he will share his joy with you again!

Lots of love,

Laura

www.ingramcontent.com/pod-product-compliance
Lightning Source LLC
Chambersburg PA
CBHW020246130626
46549CB00005B/2083